Reflections of a Wyoming Shepherd on the 23rd Psalm
Second Edition

Patricia McClaflin Booher

Rock Pavilion Press

Books Written by Patricia McClaflin-Booher

"Reflections of a Wyoming Shepherd on the 23rd Psalm"
Second Edition

"Timmy the Timid, Timmy the Tender," Tools for Coping with Grief

"Beloved Homeland," Growing up on a Wyoming Homestead

Journals

Journal for Quiet Moments

"Wyoming Roots" Writing and Planner Journal

Quilter's Writing and Design Journal

Journal of Recipes and Memories

Books to be released in the near future

"Here Lamby, Lamby, Lamby" Children's Story

Lessons of Life I learned in my Garden Patch

Creativity, "Beauty Unfolding"

© Copyright 2022

Front Cover image: Big Horn Mountain range, Photography donated
by
K.L. Reed, Shell Wyoming
All photographs within contents are from author's family album,
Unless indicated.

All rights reserved. No part of this book may be reproduced or transmitted in any form or by any means, electronic or mechanical, including photocopying, recording, or by any information storage and retrieval system without the written permission of the Publisher, except where permitted by law.
For information address: Rock Pavilion Press.

Scripture quotation is taken from the Holy Bible
New King James Version, Copyright 1982
New International Version, Copyright 1984

Printed in the United States of America

www.patriciamac.com

Rock Pavilion Press

This book is dedicated to my Grandchildren

Erik Steven Booher

John William Booher

Anna Marie Booher

Elizabeth Eileen Booher

Reagan Michael Booher

Kameron Elbert Musashi Lewis

Gabriel Josiah Isao Lewis

Perry Wallace Saburo Lewis

Luke Mitchell Ross

Maximus William Ross

Dane Atticus Ross

Claire Josephine Cook

And any future children in our family

*"All your children shall be taught by the Lord,
And great shall be the peace of your children."
Isaiah 54:13 NKJV*

ACKNOWLEDGEMENTS

It would not be possible to mention all those friends that have come along in this journey of writing in the later years of my life but I will highlight just a few.

I have dedicated this shepherd book to each of my grandchildren and those to follow, as my heart's desire is that one day they will pick up this little book and read of those life experiences that gave their grandmother courage, humor and love for living.

At the top of the list would be my children and their mates. My son and his wife are Craig and Sandy Booher. My daughters and their husbands are, Shana and Paul Lewis and Rachel and Mitch Ross.

My mother and father, Wallace and Edna Mae McClaflin gave me the roots and fiber to write this story. It was the look of pride I would see on their faces that gave me the drive and stamina to finish college degrees that have served me well. Their bold faith to build a life on virgin soil on a homestead in the northern parts of Wyoming is a heritage rich with color, integrity, and a work ethic that has followed me throughout my life.

My brothers and their wives, hands down, have loved me unconditionally. They have been my cheerleaders throughout this journey of life. My eldest brother and his wife are Mike and Linda McClaflin. My youngest brother, who towers over me, and his wife are Wayne and Pam McClaflin.

The Heart Mountain homestead community gave me a sense of place and belonging. Many of the snippets of stories in the shepherd book are from my childhood.

A cherished friend, Robin Niles has faithfully edited my grief book and now comes along side once again.

I have many "Forever Friends," and I will list some of those that have significantly made an impact on this manuscript. Ronnie and Teddy Jones gave of themselves so unselfishly, in their friendship and in allowing me to write their life's' stories as shepherds. Virla Harrell has the heart of an artist. Her dedication in transcribing the many interviews for the homestead project was a backdrop in putting together parts of this shepherd's story. Her painting of the shepherd that went to Africa will be with those children for a long time to come.

The cover picture taken atop the Big Horn Mountain range will always be cherished. KL and Linda Reed provided the photograph. They lived just down the hill there in Shell, Wyoming. KL is one of those ranchers we read about in history books. Linda, is one of my very cherished friends. Through all of my writing endeavors they were always my cheerleaders. Whenever I return to Wyoming, I always make a trek over to see my very special friends.

My oldest grandson Erik, was invaluable in helping the first time around with the shepherd book as a computer technician. I could not have published the book without him. Anna Booher, the Ross brothers, Kam and Kassie and Gabe Lewis have faithfully taken videos of the books which warms my heart. Each of my family members have played a role in encouraging me in this season of writing in the later years of my own journey. I miss my dear friends Mary Ellen Fraser and Pat Vess as they were always such encouragers all these years of writing. These dear friends gave me wings to fly with this Shepherd book. They are Phyllis and Ray Sammons, Ruth and Joe Shadler, Jessie Maurer and Sharon Talon.

I want to thank Paul, Shana's husband for designing the cover for the homestead book and restoring the old photos in the album. I know he spent countless hours and for that I will always be grateful. We both have our roots in Wyoming, so that is a double bonus in him being like a son to me.

In the last few years, I have been a part of Memoir Writer's Group that has been a proved to give me courage and tenacity to just keep writing. Each of us became kindred spirits as we patiently took the time to listen with an emphatic heart to each reading that was presented. I have come to realize, that for those of us who write, this is invaluable. I want to thank Jim and Coralie Johnson as they have faithfully given leadership to each one of us.

Mary Martin helped me take creativity to another level. Her friendship and the opportunities she gave me in attending "Quilting in the Tetons," were incredible.

If I knew that one day I would write a book on overcoming grief and that my Yorky pet would be the main character I would have taken many more pictures.

My grandson John worked very hard in creating and using Timmy's picture for the cover of "Timmy the Timid, Timmy the Tender," Tools for coping with grief.

    The years spent with UW Cooperative Extension Service were invaluable for me as I expanded and grew in so many ways. I am grateful for the doors of opportunity that were afforded me. I want to give credit to four Directors of UW Extension who helped me immensely. They are Jim Debree, Darrell Kauztmann, Edna McBreen, and Glenn Whipple. Dr. Ben Silliman and Dr. Karen Williams, UW colleagues, introduced me to Family Resiliency and Qualitative Research.

    The impact on my life as a young child in the 4-H Youth program would be a great source of endurance in this process of writing. Some of those Extension Agents were Jimmy Nichols, Neil and Edith Anderson, Harold Hurich and Lyle Bang.

    Those professors of Eastern Michigan University gave me wings to fly. Dr. Williston and Dr. Young expanded my horizons in Child Development. Dr. Found is a role model anyone would want to follow. Dr. Laws gave me layers and layers of knowledge and insight I have relied upon. Dr. Betty Barber challenged the fiber of my foundation and for that I am grateful.

There are countless other friends who have walked along side and so I must keep walking and writing and give those younger generations of writers and poets hope and a sense of destiny.

CONTENTS

Information   5

Dedication   6

Acknowledgments   7

Contents   13

Introduction   17

Chapter 1: Return to the Lambing sheds   25

Chapter 2: The Lord is my shepherd, I shall not want   33
    Lamby Stories
    The Lord is my Shepherd, I shall not want
    Teddy's introduction to the Heavenly Shepherd
    Bum Lambs
    Knowing the Shepherds care through
        Writing and Covid

Chapter 3: Green Pastures   47
    Shepherd girl
    Billy Woodruff

Chapter 4: Leads by Still Waters   59
    Lake Michigan
    Beachcomber

Chapter 5: He restores my soul   73
    The first day of the rest of my life
    Wounds of the soul
    Moonlight on the water

Chapter 6: He leads me in the paths of righteousness   89
    Feed the Chickens
    WWII
    Election year
    Eagles Eyesight

     Alfred Cawston
     4-H Tragedy
     Sunday morning trip to church
     Namesake
     Enlarge your tent

Chapter 7: Valley of the shadow of death   109
     Car wreck in Shirley Basin
     Robin Red Breast
     Death of a father
     The Pioneer Woman, My Mom

Chapter 8: Acceptance   137
     Prison visit
     Morning Stroll with my Shepherd
     Shell canyon
     Winter Rose Bud

Chapter 9: I will fear no evil   161
     What if?
     Those Moments of time with the children
     Rusty rescues Wayne
     Elk hunting trip

Chapter 10: Your rod and your staff, they comfort me 177

Chapter 11: You prepare a table for me 183
     Biscuits and cream
     You anoint my head with oil

Chapter 12: Old barns and shepherds 199
     Old Barns
     Memories of Paint Creek ranch
     4-H sewing project
     Gardening
     Shepherds

Chapter 13: Surely goodness and mercy 215
     Lambing season and school tours on the Jones farm
     The voice of the Shepherd

Chapter 14: And I will dwell in the house of the Lord forever	225
Choices	
A sense of time and place, "Community"	
Passage	
Upcoming Children's Book:	239
"Here Lamby, Lamby, Lamby"	
Family Photo Album	245
Resources	273
Book Order Information	275

INTRODUCTION

The 23rd Psalm has been a universally loved passage of scripture down through the ages. I have always tended to spend a good deal of time reading the Psalms. I seem to relate to the shepherd boy David as he would spend many long days out with the sheep.

The McClaflin family made their way to northern Wyoming in 1950 to begin life anew on the windswept prairies of northern Wyoming. It was a small homestead community that was made up of about 120 WWII veterans and their young families.

The flocks of sheep that were always a part of the McClalfin farm had begun early one spring morning when a friend, Billy Woodruff came to the front door and asked our mother if she would like to take on some bum lambs. I was very young at the time. I had no idea that in those growing up years caring for those orphan lambs and spending time out in the fields with flocks of sheep would one day evolve into being an author bringing back the many memories of those lambs I grew to love.

This is a second edition of "Reflections of a Wyoming Shepherd on the 23rd Psalm." I am now on the other side of my seventies and I cannot ever remember a time, as we are living in today. More than ever in the past, the 23rd Psalm brings with it courage, truth and a road map of destiny in times of great difficulty not only in our nation but across the world.

I don't believe anyone would have thought after all this time the Covid pandemic would still be with us but it is. Last winter I became very ill with Covid. It would take months to gain my strength back. As the days moved into weeks and then months, I felt I must complete and publish the book that was setting on my shelf in the office on coping with grief, "Timmy the Timid, Timmy the Tender, Tools for Coping with Grief." My mother had passed away just a few months before the shut-down for the pandemic. She missed being 100 years-old by just thirty-seven days. As I would hear of so many grand-parents dying alone away from family my heart would just ache.

I knew I was gravely ill, but there was such a sense of destiny still down inside of my heart, I knew I would recover. It was a difficult task, as I was still so exhausted and weary and my thoughts were muddled, but just like in countless times throughout my life, the Great Shepherd of Heaven would come along side and give me the stamina to complete the task I had been called to.

The first shepherd book was published in 2009. Day after day I would be upstairs in my office in my old vintage home looking out on the snow covered evergreens writing snippets of stories that evolved into the first non-fiction novel.

Once again, as in former times in my life, the stories are surfacing in my mind and soul. I am penning more stories of this Shepherd of Heaven who has walked along side of me all my life.

Those every day experiences of life I have written in the form of snippets or poems or even the old hymns I grew up with will not necessarily be in chronological order, but rather I have placed them in the verses of the 23rd Psalm that best describe the story.

I had begun this life of writing when I still lived in Shell, Wyoming working with the University of Wyoming Cooperative Extension. During those years I worked extensively with topics surrounding "Family Resiliency." I attended a conference on Youth Assets that encourage strong healthy families. It was the last session and I was sitting with my childhood friends who also worked in UW Extension. As we listened to the excellent speaker, it was as if each of us came to the realization at once.

We had been the best of friends growing up together in the 4-H Youth Organization. As I sat there that day a seed of hope and destiny began to grow. The seeds of courage and grit took form and the outcome was a research project, "Impact on Growing up on a Wyoming Homestead." My State Extension Director, Edna McBreen, gave a green light to pursue the research.

This Qualitative Research project became bigger than one person, as it took on a life of its own. Trying to work full time and conduct the project was impossible. The new state director encouraged me to apply for a year sabbatical. Glenn Whipple, Director of UW Cooperative Extension had called me in my Big Horn county office. I picked up the phone, and said hello. Glen got right to the point, "Patty I wanted to be the first one to tell you, we have just gotten word that you have been awarded a year sabbatical to do your research." I think I screamed in his ear. I was just beside myself, driving the car home was hard as I felt like I was flying like an eagle.

So many of the original homesteaders had already passed away, so there was an urgency to complete the research so that the documentation and book could be completed. I hadn't planned on the project getting down so deep in my heart. The interviews that were taped and transcribed were with family members, friends and neighbors who had taken a vital part in my own life growing up. My own mother was getting old and I wished more than anything to have the research and book completed for her.

The next week I would be attending the annual conference for all the Cooperative Extension faculty across the state and university specialists in Laramie, Wyoming.

It was a busy week before heading out that Sunday morning for the university which was a seven-hour trip. Some extension colleagues I would be seeing were close friends I had grown up with out on Heart Mountain homestead community. They had been my cheerleaders from the very beginnings of the research project. Life can be full of surprises and these unexpected experiences can change a person's life. I remember vividly quoting Psalm 23 and feeling a wonderful presence of God's love for me as I drove late in the afternoon on that bitter cold Sunday in February. I do not remember colliding with a snowplow. I can only recall the bone chilling blast of wind that blew into my face as I looked into the scared face of the weather-worn face of a man I had never seen. I did not realize till later, that his look of fear was because he was afraid I had been killed on impact.

I was so happy to be alive; I was not going to complain about anything but recovery was a long process. I went into the sabbatical year slowly recovering, with my strength greatly depleted. My expectation was that the project would be completely done in a year. That was not going to happen.

I kept working for the university, but the close call with eternity out in the middle of nowhere did not set with my son Craig. He wanted his mother in Michigan and he was not going to take no for an answer. Going through an experience like I did out in Shirley Basin helped me realize how quickly life can pass before us. With this realization, visiting grandchildren on holidays wasn't enough anymore.

It took a great deal of soul searching but I came to the conclusion it was time for me to retire from my position with the university. I decided to completely change careers. I moved to Michigan and became a Real Estate agent. The plan was that I would do this part time and with the extra time I would write and spend time with all those grandchildren. I took on this new challenge with gusto. Learning quickly, as I was immediately surprised at just what it meant to become a part of the Real Estate business. Days melted into weeks. Months passed so quickly, and then several years.

After a time, I found myself waking up in the night with a heavy heart; knowing I had been given more time on this earth to complete the writing and research. I was perplexed because by the time I came home many times late at night, I was too exhausted to write. Along with the exhaustion, my mind was so full of work related tasks; there was no room to come away to that quiet place the writer has to find.

So this is where I found myself on a week-end on a frigid January morning in Michigan. Families wanted to stay nestled near the warm fireplace. Looking for a new home was not a first priority for clients. As was my custom I was enjoying a strong cup of coffee sitting on the couch with my little Yorky type dog, Timmy. I was saying my morning prayers and reading the Bible. Thoughts began to surface. I turned to Psalm 23. I read it over, line by line. I hurried upstairs to my office, turned on the computer, and began to write what was coming so rapidly to me. Childhood experiences with the lambs out in the sheep barn came back with intensity. And with the writing came a soulful weeping from the depths of me. What was I to do with this? I couldn't take on a new writing project now, as the homestead research was like a heavy weight on my shoulders.

I would wake up in the night, my mind full of thoughts of this Great Shepherd of Heaven, Jesus Christ. The drive within me could not be dismissed. That was the beginning of the story of a shepherd girl growing up in the northern plains of Wyoming.

After some time, I knew I would need to put full time into the writing and research. One afternoon I walked into my broker's office and told Bob Sonsara I needed to put my license in escrow and spend full time on the writing and research. He said, "Why don't you just work part time?" I knew what I needed to do." This was going to be a great challenge of faith for me, but I had been down this road of pure courage many times in my life.

I can't remember when I began to love this Great Shepherd of Heaven, but I grew up with a sense that He walked very close to me, speaking to me on the wind, and in the quiet of the sheep barns. In my journey of life, I have found many other persons who have not had the privilege of knowing this Shepherd, Jesus Christ. The drive and passion that has brought this story of life living on a homestead in northern Wyoming into focus is because I have come to love this Shepherd of Heaven so dearly. I think often of fellow travelers who have lost their way or me have never had the opportunity to know this kind and loving shepherd from Heaven.

"My people have been lost sheep; their shepherds have led them astray and caused them to roam on the mountains. They wandered over mountain and hill and forgot their own resting place."
Jeremiah 50:6

That first winter of the Covid pandemic I was able to complete the homestead book, "Beloved Homeland, Growing up on a Wyoming Homestead." One would think I should just take a rest, but as I look about and see the sorrow and desperation of so many, I find myself asking, in this season of my life, when I am getting much older, what can I do to make a difference? Since the first shepherd book was published, I have lived through so many experiences that have only increased my faith and resilient spirit of a young homestead shepherd girl.

Once I again I find myself sitting here at my desk penning those words of life and how very rich it is. In this season of my life, I am living in a cottage on the lake and for a writer that is a blessing of pure joy. It is again early January with the beautiful lake incased in a heavy layer of ice, but I am warm, at great peace and full of many stories of life to share.

Let me take your hand and let us journey together back into the lambing sheds and walk across newly plowed fields on a Wyoming homestead. May I have the privilege of introducing you to this Shepherd in Psalm 23?

Psalm 23

The Lord is my shepherd,
I shall not want.
He makes me to lie down in green pastures;
He leads me in the path of righteousness
For his name's sake.
Yea, though I walk through the valley of the shadow of death I will fear no evil;
For You are with me;
Your rod and Your staff, they comfort me.
You prepare a table before me in the presence of my enemies;
You anoint my head with oil.
Surely goodness and mercy shall follow me
All the days of my life;
And I will dwell in the house of the Lord Forever.
NKJV

CHAPTER 1

RETURNING TO THE LAMBING SHEDS

The January winter had set in and the Christmas holidays were but a memory now. The grandchildren's quilts had been completed just in time. The children took delight in seeing the smiling faces of cartoon characters looking back at them from the quilting patches sewed with a great deal of love. All the sewing supplies and boxes of fabric had been taken back to the basement and the New Year was upon us with all its expectations. It seems I move back and forth with quilting, designing, and then I come full circle into that place of writing which takes a great deal of self-discipline.

A team was evolving within our congregation in preparation for a mission trip to Kenya, East Africa in June of 2008. The projects that would be a part of this trip would be to build a roof and foundation for a church in Kisumu. During the day and evenings we would conduct services along with a Children's Crusade.

I have always enjoyed working with children. I was given permission to write and prepare stories for the Children's Crusade. The African children would be very acquainted with lambs, so I began wring a Lamby story and making puppets as well.

As I prepared myself for this endeavor something began to burn within me. I found myself returning time and again to Psalm 23. This particular Psalm is universal as it reaches across all denominations and beliefs. I had grown up loving the words of this chapter of the Bible.

The impact on my life of the power in the words would forever be as a seal on my heart after quoting it over and over just before a catastrophic car wreck in a snowstorm out in Shirley Basin in Wyoming in February of 2001 while traveling to the University of Wyoming for a conference.

Those of us northern dwellers begin the count down in the early parts of January marking off the weeks of winter.

For a nature lover like myself, I welcome the cold days as it is a wonderful time to write. Now that I can look out from my French doors in my office on a frozen lake, I feel I am doubly blessed.

That cold January when those first thoughts of writing of the 23rd Psalm are but a memory now. I do remember being perplexed at those thoughts in the night of the 23rd Psalm as the research was still not completed and the years seemed to be slipping by much too quickly.

This silent voice of God that has followed me throughout my own journey here on the earth came night after night. I finally just had to lay it all down and begin to write. As I tried to go back to childhood memoires it was evident I had been away from the lamby barns too long.

Friends from childhood, Ronnie and Teddy Jones still lived on the homestead. They had raised sheep all of their lives and it was the beginning of the lambing season.

Our families were neighbors out on the Heart Mountain Homestead community. Both families raised sheep. Teddy and I spent many years growing up together in 4-H and we were the greatest of friends.

It was because of Teddy that I came back to Wyoming. She had told Jim Debree, the former Director of the University of Wyoming Cooperative Extension, about me. I was contacted out in Oregon, where I lived at the time. My job application was accepted and I took a position as a Family Consumer Science Educator. Because I had grown up in a family involved in the 4-H program, I once again came along the 4-H agents assisting in the work of the 4-H program. Teddy and I worked together in a number of trainings and with the county and state fairs. So once again I had renewed a friendship that had begun in childhood.

One evening after a long day of working, I went to my home computer and began writing the stories of my childhood experiences with the sheep. I pulled out references for information I needed. There was nothing to do but go back and spend some time in the lambing barns.

I called Teddy and Ronnie Jones during the lambing season which usually began in the middle of January.

I had job obligations so it wasn't possible for me to fly to Wyoming until March. Teddy was concerned as the lambing season would be over by that time.

I contacted my mother who still lived on the Heart Mountain homestead and my brother Wayne and his wife Pam, who live on the McClaflin farm across the road.

My friend, Virla Harrell had been transcribing all the taped interviews with the homesteaders, so she had grown to be very acquainted with this Heart Mountain homestead community. My enthusiasm for spending days in the sheep barns must have been contagious, for as I told Virla of my plans, she wanted to come along and finally get to see the mountain she had heard so much about, visible from the homestead.

I had many job obligations, so I worked feverishly to be able to take some days away, booked a flight and met Virla at the Denver airport. We spent the day preparing for the drive to Wyoming the next day. We were up at dawn and off we went across the prairies of Wyoming on Interstate 25. We drove up over the Big Horn mountain range on highway 14. As I was again seeing the beauty of the switchbacks on the western slope, I was in awe of my old stomping ground.

Our time was limited, but I just couldn't drive across Wyoming without driving down through Shell canyon and stopping to see KL and Linda Reed. There really aren't words to express the beauty of the Big Horn mountain range. The artist in Virla would have to see it for herself. We stopped at the cattle bridge, a place I had visited often while living in Shell. It was so good to see my dear friends. The minutes ticked by too quickly, and then we were off to see my family waiting out on the homestead.

I have cherished the photograph given to me, taken by KL Reed. It is on the cover of the shepherd book. It was taken in a meadow at the top of the Big Horn Mountain range.

Homestead women know how to cook like no other. Mom had a hearty meal ready for us. Wayne and Pam came over that first night and excitement was in the air for this project that had been placed so deep inside my heart from a lifetime of knowing this Shepherd, described in Psalm 23.

I had been calling Teddy every few days, hoping there would still be lambs being born when we arrived. The lambing season had come to a close. I was greatly disappointed, for as the time came closer to being out in sheep barns again, I wanted the thrill of watching a newborn lamb with its mother.

The next morning was a typical early March morning, cold and windy. In fact the winds could be described as brutal that day. The clear cerulean sky overhead had winds that sounded like a freight train rumbling over the plains. It was unnerving as Virla, Mom and I got out of the car. Here came Teddy with that wonderful smile, bucket in hand out of the gate. Her hugs were always like a small mother bear, and now I would be able to introduce two of my special friends.

The excitement was contagious; it was as if each of us shared a mission from on high. Teddy's face was radiant, "Patty I have a surprise for you." My heart pounded hard, "Oh Teddy what is it?"

"We had a set of triplets born this morning!"

I wanted to run out to the barn right then, but Teddy needed to put part of the lunch in the oven. I went to the farmhouse with her, paced around the living room, wanting to get out in the barns. Ronnie had been called, as he had gone out early in the morning to begin plowing in preparation for spring planting.

And then we all went together, tape recorder in hand, out to the sheep sheds. There in the lambing pen with fresh straw laid out were three beautiful new lambs.

The mother was a beautiful Suffolk ewe with black face. There were two black lambs and one white with black spots on his face. The spotted faced lamb would be named Sammy and he would be used as a narrator for the children's story.

This was an answer to prayer, for I had asked the Lord if it could be possible for a late lamb to be born while we were on the

Jones farm. God with his wonderful humor sent us three lambs' just hours before we arrived.

Ronnie came out to the barn, and we walked around taking pictures, and trying as best we could to glean the wisdom from Teddy and Ronnie.

They are shepherds with hearts that love the flocks of sheep that God has entrusted them with. Teddy introduced Virla and I to Nathan Splitstone, he is a shepherd who works at the Jones farm, helping with the many flocks. He was a great help to us with taking the pictures of the lambs.

We liked his hat, as it looked like a well-worn large brimmed design that spoke of many life stories.

At noon we went back to the house and Teddy introduced Virla and me to a black Suffolk lamb and a white Columbia lamb. The black-faced lamb would be named "Bo," and the white-faced lamb would be named Susie. While caring for the ewes and lambs, Ronnie had found Bo with an open sore. He didn't know what had happened, but he had brought the little lamb to the farmhouse for Teddy to nurse back to health.

Sometimes a ewe will not receive her lamb and this was the case for Susie. Her mother had crushed her ribs and broken her back leg. Susie was also brought to the house and cared for with loving hands.

The work required to care for hundreds of sheep begins early in the morning, and sometimes can go throughout the night. The sheep sheds were a busy place, but also the farm house was filled with activity. Teddy would care for Susie and Bo throughout the day.

Farm women cook meals that are hardy, so Mom was in the kitchen often helping Teddy preparing the next meal. That first morning after the feeding was done, Ronnie came into the house. We sat down at the dining room table, I sat up the tape recorder and the interviews began. I went down through the chapter, verse by verse. After a few minutes, I relaxed, ask very few questions, and listened to a shepherd with the heart of a pastor. After lunch was over, and

Teddy was free to be interviewed, I was again taken with the nurturing heart of a woman who had a deep love for God.

When it was time to feed the bum lambs, I felt like I had come back home to my roots. Throughout the stories of Psalm 23, I will share excerpts of the wisdom and description of the nature and life of sheep given by Teddy and Ronnie in our many conversations which were taped. The trip came to an end too quickly and then it was time to drive back to Longmont, Colorado, where Virla lives with her husband Gordy. It was early in the morning; we hugged Mom, Pam, and my tall handsome brother Wayne and we were off for the nine hour drive across Wyoming.

Virla got out her paints, and while I drove, she painted a picture of Ronnie holding the little lamb named Sammy.

Neither of us realized, on that day, that the picture of a gentle Shepherd holding his lamb would make its way across continents to be in the hands of many African children in just a few months. As I flew home the next morning, there was an excitement, as to just where and what was happening with the stories that were coming from life experiences.

When I was back in my home office at the computer, the stories began to take form about Sammy, Bo and Susie. Early on I realized these stories of the lambs would be going to Africa with the team. As I worked way into the nights, day after day, the pictures of African children would formulate in my mind. I will speak of this in the chapters to come as I tell of how the depth of life's richness was penned on the page in the next few weeks, and I was blessed.

This season of life, watching my grown children and enjoying grandchildren is a blessed time. I realize my childhood growing up on a Wyoming homestead is rare in today's society. The wisdom I gained from the times I spent out on my horse Snip riding over hills and dales, seeing the massive rocky mountain ranges close by has given a measure of richness to my life. Those times working along with my family out in the sheep barns and feeding bum lambs has given treasured memories.

Teddy and Ronnie have lived out their lives calling in being Godly shepherds to the flocks of sheep entrusted to them. Throughout this tender story, I will share with you many life experiences of my own, as well as the wisdom of these shepherds who have been so kind to open their hearts to you.

CHAPTER 2
The Lord is my Shepherd I Shall not Want

When I was planning the short trip to Wyoming, I was grateful for the many experiences that had been afforded me, during the many Qualitative Research interviews I had conducted in regard to the Heart Mountain Homestead project. During that research I was still working with the University of Wyoming, so I had many resources I could tap into from professors who conducted this type of research. Rick Ewig, Director of UW American Heritage Center, had been a valuable colleague in the research project. I had read books on how to conduct qualitative research, as I felt a great desire to do the best I possibly could. The community where I conducted the research was where I had my roots and I felt a great deal of commitment to those homesteaders. When I first began going into homes to conduct interviews, I would be so anxious, but after a while I learned to relax. I had a check list for myself and supply bag with everything I could possibly need. There were specific questions I would ask each family, but after they had been answered, I would just sit back and let the family members tell their life story.

So now here I was again about to interview family members and friends from childhood. Teddy and Ronnie had both spent a lifetime on the farm. The day to day experiences with raising sheep had given them an understanding about life, not often found in the urban society of today. This was not just a job. After walking through the barns and watching how they cared for their flocks of sheep, it was apparent that being a shepherd of flocks of sheep was a God ordained appointment for this couple.

After the interviews had been transcribed something became very apparent. As I read over the accounts of parts and pieces of the 23rd Psalm from the eyes of earthly shepherds, I was made aware of the wisdom and enlightenment of scripture that is conveyed by these fellow sojourners walking this path with God.

Ron and Teddy Jones on their sheep farm

LAMBY STORIES

I had returned home with a grateful heart, knowing the time with family and close friends had been like a breath of Heaven. There had been such a sacrifice of time and energy given to Virla and me in those few days on the old homestead. Now it was time for me to pen on page the stories that were formulating in my mind.

Those little lambs out in the sheep barns had gotten down into my heart. It was if I had gone back to my roots as a child caring for the lambs. I would check with Teddy every few days to see how Bo was recovering. One evening she had to tell me he had died. I couldn't believe it. "What happened Teddy?"

"I don't know, he seemed to be getting stronger, but I went to town, and when I came back he was lying on the mat next to the front door. I knew something was wrong because Susie was running all over the yard, crying baa, baa, and then running back to Bo."

When I got off the phone, I felt terrible. What was the matter with me? It was a sick little bum lamb I would never see again anyway, but I was so disappointed. With the news of Bo dying, the faces of little African children were center focus in my thoughts as I would write. At times I was overcome with weeping, I would have to stop for a time, and then begin writing again.

I would reflect on a time just a few years prior when I was out in the middle of badlands in Wyoming with brutal winds blowing into my car that was crushed all around me. I had to wait for an hour for an ambulance to come and help me. I wasn't afraid, just bone chilling cold. And now I was thinking about those little children in desperate situations. Were they afraid, as many of them had already watched their parents die of terrible diseases? The Shepherd of Heaven would whisper to me in the night, "Take the 23rd Psalm to these children of mine across the oceans."

The day Virla and I drove back across Wyoming from spending time in the sheep barns; she was painting a picture of Ronnie out in the barnyard with the triplet Sammy in his arms. We decided the picture would be a shadow with words of the 23rd Psalm overlaid. When we arrived in Longmont we went to see a graphic artist, David Nelson who had worked with Virla on other projects. It took some time to describe what we had visualized, but we finally were happy with the outcome.

One Sunday morning as I drove to church, I stopped at a red light. It just came to me in an instant. It was a picture in my mind. It would take some investigation, but I was determined. I needed to locate the 23rd Psalm written in Swahili. Both the English and Swahili version would be placed as an overlay of the lamby picture with Ronnie.

My brother Mike and his wife Linda had been missionaries in Africa for twenty years. Later he became the Regional Area Director of all of Africa for the Assembly of God denomination. He and his wife Linda would take many trips to countries all over Africa. Mike is one of my heroes, but then Linda is an incredible human being in her own right. She was the one who always had the gift for writing. The Lord gave her a special appointment.

Across Africa, every year all the two-hundred Assembly of God missionary wives knew they would receive a personal birthday card with a hand written message from Linda. I knew they would be the best source in finding the Swahili version for the 23rd Psalm. I was excited about the inlaid picture. When I told Linda we were going to pass them out to the children, she said, "Be careful, you will be mobbed with the children." I did not have a context for what she was telling me, but our mission team would soon find out.

The picture was sized down so four copies would fit on a page. Virla wanted to contribute to the missions endeavor so she had a thousand copies made. A group of volunteers from our church helped to laminate the pictures. We cut them out with a hole at the top, and inserted yarn that would fit over a small child's head.

The final preparations for the mission trip were completed and the team was ready to head out. As each member pulled on their back pack, they were given a large plastic bag containing those little pictures of the Wyoming shepherd.

The mission team was met at the Nairobi International airport by Debbie and David Barthalow. David was a building contractor from the states. He and Debbie had felt a divine call to go to Africa to oversee the building of churches. Before the week was over, every team member would not only love this couple, but would have the greatest respect for both of them, as the dedication they possess is an act of God's grace.

They took us to the mission compound to regroup, take showers, and get ready to head out to Kisumu. We drove by the home where my brother's family had lived when I had visited them several times years before. Pastor Rachel had connected with her Uncle Mike so that our mission trip would coincide with one of his and Linda's many trips to Africa. So it was with excitement and tears concealed, that I saw them drive up. We had lunch with them and then they were off with a full schedule.

As we loaded up and headed south across the riff valley, I became anxious. What about these lamby stories? Would the children understand about sheep? And so my fretting along with jet lag came over me.

As we drove along the highway looking down in the valley, the sights and sounds and aromas of Africa came back to me. I had many special memories of spending time with my brother's family from years past.

As I looked out over the side of the road I began to see sheep tied up so they could graze along the highway. That first morning when we were taken to the job sight I saw herdsmen with flocks of sheep.

The children's crusade was to be conducted in the late afternoon, as the missions team could not stay on the work sight after dark, because of safety issues, and there were no exceptions. The first night, after the lamby stories had been told and Pastor Rachel preached, we began to hand out the laminated picture of Sammy and the 23rd Psalm. By the second night, Linda's warning came to pass. Hundreds of children were mobbing the team handing out the pictures. One of the tall African pastors took the large bag, held it high above his head, and ran across the dirt road, the mobs of children running after him. It was such a funny sight, we laughed a great deal over it. At the same time, realizing these children had nothing of material value, this little picture was a treasure to them. They would be thrilled during the day, as the men would give them the empty water bottles. This would become a toy they would play with all day. The little laminated picture could be seen hanging around their small necks.

By the third night, the team had gotten organized with the help of the African pastors. After service the children were lined up and we would go as quickly as possible down the lines handing out the lamby picture. The Great Shepherd of Heaven finds all children precious in his sight, and he knew just what would bless them. Long after we had returned home, I am sure the children wore the inscription of the 23rd Psalm around their necks. I prayed often that it would be a reminder to them, that they were loved and the Lord can take fear out of the heart of the smallest child.

It was so hard to leave the children every evening. There were so many of them crowding around us, that I would just put my hand on their heads and bless them in Jesus name. The vans would be loaded, darkness setting in, "Where is Mama Craig.?" I would be out in the midst of the children. It is customary for mother's to be addressed with the name of the first born, so thus Craig was my eldest child, so I would be addressed as Mama Craig.

The mission team handing out the lamby picture in Kenya, East Africa

Just two years later, there would be a terrible uprising in that area of Kenya and some of the church members were brutally murdered. I just have to trust that the little picture with the 23rd Psalm inscription was an avenue for the life changing words of the Bible to find a resting place in the many children we quickly learned to love.

A great deal of thought went into the story about the lambs we encountered those few days in Wyoming with Teddy and Ronnie. The story that came out of the situations with the triplet named Sammy who was used as the narrator, Susie the Columbia lamb and Bo the Suffolk lamb are not so different than one would find among persons we walk along with in everyday life. It was decided that there would be two books written about the 23rd Psalm. "Reflections of a Wyoming Shepherd on the 23rd Psalm," and the orphan lamb story would become a children's story. I couldn't decide what the title would be for the children's book. One morning while setting in the quiet dawning of day, I remembered Teddy as she would go out to the barns and feed her bum lambs. With a big heavy bucket full of bottles of warm milk, she would call out, "Here Lamby, Lamby, Lamby."

"That's it!" Later that morning, I called Teddy. When I told her I had come up with a title, she wanted to hear it. "Well Teddy, how does this sound? "Here Lamby, Lamby, Lamby." I could almost see the smile break out on her face over the phone line.

THE LORD IS MY SHEPHERD

When did I first meet the Great Shepherd from Heaven? I have had this question put to me many times. Going back to my first thoughts of God cannot be placed in a specific time frame, as I think I have had a realization of him from the time I was very small. Our family went to church, and I can remember Mom reading the Bible to Mike and me when we were preschoolers. She told of how she had received Christ when she was eighteen.

My Grandmother Hannah Brown had a deep love for God and I always felt very close to her. I didn't get to see her very often, but I connected with her, knowing I had a special place in her heart. Grandpa and Grandma Brown lived in Gage, Oklahoma. When I was in the fifth grade, our family went to see them for the holidays. Grandpa Brown was very sick at the time, and had to stay in bed. I always knew Mom loved him very dearly. Dad's sister lived in Forgan, so a few days after Christmas Daddy took Mike and they drove to see his family. I stayed behind with Mom, as she wanted to spend more time with her parents. The day she said good-bye to her Dad, my heart ached for her as she felt this would be the last time she would see him. As we drove away, I somehow knew what she was feeling was true, and in March he passed away.

Our Heart Mountain community still did not have phone service, so very dear family friends, Bessie and Felix Hoff were called. It was late at night when they drove out from Powell to give Mom the news. I was supposed to be asleep, but I lay quietly and listened to them. I heard Mom begin to cry and with her weeping a great sense of loss came to me for a Grandpa's smile that we would never see again. She traveled to Oklahoma for the funeral and while there she had an encounter with God that would change the destiny of our family.

A few days later when I came home on the school bus I was happy as I walked into the house and saw Mom standing in the kitchen. As soon as I saw her, I sensed something different about her. "What has happened to you Mom?"

She took me back to her bedroom and set me down on the bed. As she began to tell me what happened to her, I began to cry. I had been praying for some time to be closer to God, and as she spoke God answered my prayers. I asked Christ to come into my heart and become my Savior on that day, and I have loved him from that day on. I think I have always loved God, but on that afternoon setting next to my mother, in a state of grief over the loss of her father, the Great Shepherd became my Savior.

The 23rd Psalm begins with the first verse, "The Lord is my shepherd." The word "my" describes a shepherd who loves each of us in a personnel way. It was as if a warm and bright light was turned on in my soul that day and prayer became very important in my life. I looked forward to the times that I could ride my horse out in the hills and on those days I was very aware of God's presence all around me.

In those months after Grandpa passed away we attended a small Assembly of God church. There was an alter that stretched across the front of the sanctuary. After Sunday evening service I would go up to the front of the church and kneel down by my pastor's wife, Sister Thiemann. The experiences I had during those times as a young girl at the altar, have given me a foundation of God's love for me in a personal way that has given the faith and determination to walk with God all of my life.

I certainly am not perfect. As the years pass, I realize more and more how much I need God's strength moment by moment.

Throughout my life, when I have made mistakes and sinned, my heart has been so broken, because I discover as I take a diverging path, I do not feel as close to God, so I have always turned around and run back into his arms. It is amazing to think that this same God who spoke from a burning bush to Moses, gave songs to the Shepherd boy David while out tending flocks, would come and love a little shepherd girl out in the lambing sheds of Wyoming.

Throughout the Bible, sheep have been used as a metaphor for the nature of man. As I look over the list in the animal kingdom, I can't help but wish we humans could have gone to a little higher rung on the ladder of intelligence and self-preservation. But alas I will have to say from experiences out in the sheep barns with bum lambs and out in the pasture with stubborn old ewes, I do see some similarities to those of us who consider ourselves human.

The good news for each of us is that finding this Shepherd is the most wonderful experience anyone could have. If one were to ask a person who has spent a lifetime walking with this God of Heaven, the response would undoubtedly be similar to mine.

Some of the special pleasures in writing this manuscript were the interviews with Teddy and Ronnie. Throughout the chapters you the reader will also recognize the deep felt passion of these followers of Christ.

I think one of the great thrills of life is to watch those special friends from childhood, as they enter into this experience of knowing the Heavenly Shepherd in a personal way. As I sat across from Teddy listening to her, I was blessed.

Teddy's Introduction to the Heavenly Shepherd

Teddy began her story. "My walk with Christ had a long time coming. I'm like Moses; I was 40 years probably in the desert. Yet way down deep as I went through life I realized that the thing that was so weak and lacking in my life was my spiritual side. I knew that something had to be done.

Like so many people I didn't have the time or the energy to devote to God and what needed to be done or how to do it. Yet I knew that someday when I had more time and energy that was an area I needed to really address and to work on.

In my mind and down deep I always knew that God was there for me and yet I was not willing to give back to God or let Him control my life. Then it all happened.

Teddy feeding bum lambs

God has interesting ways of working. I had worked as a UW 4-H Extension Agent for about 27 years. A major change came to my life during a county fair time when things were not going well. I received a phone call and God spoke to me. I think it was just like a light bulb turned on; it was time for me to shift gears and to do something else. I went and talked to my husband Ronnie about retiring. I knew it was time I turned in my retirement and marched on. And as I did I knew down very deep in my heart that I was to grow spiritually and start walking with God. And that is what I did. I got into a tremendous Bible study that turned my life around. I learned to read the Bible daily. I have learned to take God's Word and apply it to my life. I have a heartfelt commitment to being a servant of God so that I can bring God honor and glory.

I have found a contentment that is beyond understanding and with that comes much joy. He has blessed me with all that plus all my friends. I can just look back over my career and I can see God's hand and how he protected me and how he guided me and how he blessed me without me even knowing it and was so patient with me. Now I hope that I can be His servant and give back for those many years that He cared for me and loved me and is still doing the same. I hope I can bring Him the honor and glory of being His servant."

Teddy and Ronnie have spent a lifetime in caring for sheep, but it has been many years since I have had that privilege. Many techniques of feeding are much more scientific then when I was a child, but oh so many memories have surfaced as I have once again returned to my roots

Bum Lambs

My first recollection of bum lambs and how they have affected my life began to unfold as I would be teaching an adult Sunday school class in the Detroit area in the early 80s. It seemed as the city would go on forever. There were times, I would break away from a hectic schedule and drive for endless miles to find myself finally out in the country, just hoping I could see a sheep somewhere out in the pasture. Would I ever be out on the farm again, as the memory of another time came to mind?

Our three children were pushing on to the mark of their teen-years. I had gone back to college to finish a degree in secondary education. Days were filled with many things, and there wasn't much time for personal reflection, as I strived to meet the demands of life.

It was a large adult Sunday school class. I didn't know all of the students well, but I recognized all of their faces. I guess I would describe myself as a down home type, living life many times very practically with what my growing up years would describe as having a lot of horse sense.

Regardless of the Bible topic, the stories would come to me standing there in front of persons who were very dear to my heart. There was a storehouse of memories from childhood tucked away from years of taking care of bum lambs, better recognized to readers as orphan lambs.

I would spend a great deal of time in preparation, but as the lesson would begin, the passion from within me would surface. The surprise to me was, not so much the women in the audience, but the men. These were not wimpy men, but hard working fellows who thrived in the Michigan winter elements. When I taught, I would always seek for eye contact. I now call them my lamby stories, but in those days as my childhood experiences out in the sheep shed came up from inside of me, men throughout the audience would be moved to tears. This was a surprise to me, thinking everyone had some semblance of what I had taken for granted all my life of those stories tucked away in my back pocket.

As life unravels at one's feet, the divergent paths along the way sometimes are a great surprise, and many times the path is down through some fairly deep valleys. I would never have dreamed that my greatest passion in life would be writing. But here I am now with a gentle peace in my soul recalling the lambs from so long ago.

As I look back over my personal journey with this Shepherd of Heaven, there are some pivotal points that I know, without a doubt, his hand of protection covered my life.

The Shepherd's Care through Writing and Covid

The beautiful thing about those life experiences when we learn just how true this Shepherd of Heaven is, comes when we have long periods of being alone and in sickness. I will write about this in later chapters, but when I was in flight coming home from my mother's funeral, I knew I would just have to retire from my work and finish the homestead book. I was grieved that it had not been published before her death as she had so longed for that.

I had to make a quick turnaround for Christmas. There would be no quilts made for this holiday. In January, I had resigned from my job, and was ready to dive into the publishing, and from past experience I knew it would be a big task. Everything changed for everyone when the lock-down came with Covid. I had planned on help from my grandson Erik, as he had been a most valuable asset when I had written the shepherd book. I was so out of my league as I am not high tech. When I called him, he said, "Grandma I am so afraid I might give you something as I have to be out and about."

What was I going to do? Well, just like in so many times in the past, I prayed over every new challenge. Oh yes, there were times I would work way into the night, and then would realize, I had not stopped to pray over that particular task. You might ask, "Does God really care, about those everyday happenings in a persons' life?" Oh yes he cares, he is just waiting for us to come to him as he cares even about those hairs on our head. It was a happy day when the homestead book was in print. I don't know that I can really express how God walked before me but I just have to give him the Glory.

I so hoped I could get through this difficult time without Covid, but I did become so very ill for a long span of time. I not only felt the presence of my Heavenly Shepherd, but I just know that there were many ministering angels near my bed side. It was a slow process, but I was able to finish the grief book, as my heart ached for so many family members who had to die alone. So yes, I can say without a doubt, "The Lord is my shepherd, I shall not want."

CHAPTER 3
Green Pastures

"He makes me to lie down in green pastures;"
Psalm 23:2

As I read over the interview with Ronnie, transcribed from that special trip to Wyoming, I was struck with his insight and how much he sounded like a pastor. I would say he is a man of few words, but it was apparent he had spent a good deal of time thinking over what he would say to me. As I sat there that day going over each verse of the 23rd Psalm, I asked Ronnie about feeding sheep and how the food is digested.

"Sheep have three stomachs. The first stomach is where the sheep eats her food which is usually roughage but it can be grain. The food goes into the first stomach and then the sheep rests peacefully. While resting the sheep rechews the food it has eaten. This helps with digestion. After the food has been rechewed it passes into the second stomach. The sheep will spend a good deal of time resting and chewing which is termed chewing their cud. This is the second time the food has been chewed. The sheep looks peaceful and then will chew, chew, and chew. After a while this food is swallowed, the sheep will belch some more food, and the chewing process will begin again. The sheep is at peace when she is chewing her cud.

When sheep are at peace and are not hungry they are content. Psalm 23 says that sheep will lie down in green pastures. Sheep lie down and rest. Especially during the long part of the day, they like to rest and chew their cud. Now if they have had dry feed that doesn't give them a lot of nutrition, they are not going to be at peace. The flock is going to move a lot more because they are looking for food. As a good shepherd we need to bring them lush green pastures so that they can be at peace and have plenty to eat and not have to roam so far to get what they want."

SHEPHERD GIRL

There are so many memories that seem to surface in these later years of my life relating to those flocks of sheep on the McClaflin farm. How true that just like those sheep from so long ago, you and I need a shepherd watching over our lives. One would think that after a period of years we would no longer need the loving care of our Heavenly Shepherd, but as my own life passes by so quickly now, I am much aware that I need his watchful eye moment by moment. That only causes me to love my Heavenly Father more. One day when I have completed my race here on earth, what pure joy it will be to see him face to face.

Here is a small example of one of those days I so needed my father's love. It was a late August day on that hot summer afternoon on the north pasture of the Wyoming homestead. In those early years in my young twelve-year-old child's mind I did not see myself as that shepherd girl so depicted in the painting placed over my head board on my bed. The young girl holding a staff, dressed in a faded blue cotton dress has her gaze watching over the flock of sheep. Thus, it was this image in which I found myself that day so long ago.

Why are the details of that day so keenly pressed on my memory now as I near my 80 years of living here on this earth?

The field of third cutting of alfalfa had been drenched in the night with heavy rain fall. A heavy barbed wire fence divided the two fields protecting the sheep from the dangers of alfalfa, as it would cause the stomachs of the sheep to quickly swell and explode bringing rapid and tortuous death.

The lush green leaves of the alfalfa plants were an enticement to the flock of sheep I was in charge of that day. The unsuspecting sheep could not possibly have realized the danger that lay just on the other side of the barbed wire.

I remember at times my father would amusingly mention how he could recognize the personalities of the congregation of people he would observe in his own flocks of sheep out in the barn yards.

Rusty was the amazing sheep dog that I often used in my times of herding and guarding the sheep; but Rusty was a one man dog and that was my father. He would be great help unless he caught sight of my father. One stubborn old ewe headed for the fence with six followers close behind. I began to run to stop them calling for Rusty to head them off. Unfortunately for me, clear back at the house, my father stepped out on the back porch. Off ran Rusty to the house which left me to try and herd the sheep back to safety. It was too late as the sheep had quickly gathered a mouth full of wet hay before I managed to get them back into the north pasture.

It seemed to my horror of the moment, I could see the sheep's stomachs begin to swell as they cried out in anguish. My father brought a long knife with him as he quickly came out to the field. If the stomach can quickly be punctured, sometimes it can release the gas that was forming that would bring sudden death. It was a long way out to the north pasture. Six ewes had already died before he could reach me.

One of the many reasons I have had such a deep love for my father, is that in those times like that afternoon, he would just hold me until I could subside from the sobbing and distress of my broken heart watching with agony as I could not help those sheep that lay dying. I am sure it has taught me throughout my own life that in those times I needed those strong arms of an earthly shepherd father, I could feel those arms of the Great Shepherd of all humanity who is my Heavenly father.

I believe the wisdom of a father who spent so many years out in the sheep barns taking the time to observe the many personalities of those flocks of sheep he cared for found many similarities to the human frame.

It is such a reminder in one's love for humanity. We can love, pray and encourage those we love so deeply, but in the end of it all, each of us are really the only ones that can choose the path we take in life. I often find that I turn to this scripture as it sums up a good way to live one's own life. The opposite choice of the words in this verse is to be full of pride and self-will.

He has shown you, O man, what is good;

And what does the Lord require of you

But to do justly; To love mercy,

And to walk humbly with your God.

Micah 6:8 NKJV

I dare say as I write today, the words of a shepherd who was my earthly father had a keen sense of wisdom of living as he observed those flocks under his care out in the sheep barns ever so long ago. In those many experiences of growing up out with the sheep flocks, my life has been enriched in so many ways and for that I am most thankful.

One of the gifts that is most precious that was given to Mike, Wayne and me as we grew up was the love of nature. Our parents loved life on the homestead, but the special bonus was being surrounded on all sides by the great and mighty Rocky Mountains. Even after studying a topographical map, it is hard to fathom just how vast the wilderness areas are on the mountain ranges. As I reflect over the words spoken by Ronnie, a true shepherd of sheep, I recount the many times I would stand gazing out over high mountain pasture lands with bands of sheep in sight. Without the influence of Billy Woodruff, I wonder if our family would have become involved in the raising of sheep? He had bands of sheep that would be transported every summer up into the highlands of northern Wyoming wilderness. The life of the shepherds caring for these many hundreds of sheep was one of solitude. They lived in small sheep wagons which would be moved from place to place as the sheep required new and fresh pasture lands.

BILLY WOODRUFF

After spending the day in the sheep sheds with Ronnie and Teddy, Virla and I went back to the homestead with Mom. I wanted her to reflect on of some her many memories in those early years of homesteading, so we got out the tape recorder and began. One of the highlights for our family was when we went with Billy Woodruff on a fishing trip, so I wanted Mom to tell the story.

"Billy invited us many times to go with him up into the Beartooth Mountain range, up high where his sheep were taken for summer pasture. Finally one year, Wallace said, "Okay we're going to take three days and go." I remember the kids were so excited.

Before we left, I asked Billy if he wanted me to take some lemonade. He looked at me like I was nuts. It was primitive up in the mountains and we just drank water as there was nothing fancy about that trip.

So off we went way up into the Beartooth mountain range next to lakes where there were no roads. We slept in his sheep wagons and would ride on horseback before dawn to the most wonderful fishing spots. Patty can still remember eating those trout with the red fins and how delicious they were. In the evening we would come into camp and the men would get a big fire going and fry up the fish with fried potatoes. In the morning Billy fixed sourdough pancakes with bacon and eggs. In the evening, after supper, we would set around the camp fire and Billy would tell us some of the most outlandish stories about the early years in Wyoming.

When Billy caught his first fish, he cut off the red fin and that is what we used for bait. Everyone caught fish. We would ride horses way back to deep blue mountain lakes along deer paths. It was high in the mountains, so the sun rays were intense. We would begin at four in the morning to load up and ride for a long distance. We would be tired at night, but we all enjoyed being with Billy so much.

Afterward we were so glad that we decided to go because that winter he found out he had cancer, and passed away. I believe he was eighty-one. Such a nice fellow, we missed him so much, as we always had enjoyed the times he would stop by the house for a cup of coffee or a meal."

I am grateful I have my mother's voice on tape, and the words she spoke in transcript form. The trip to the Beartooth Mountains with Billy Woodruff is a highlight in our family's collection of memories. I can still remember the fun of catching the brookies in those icy cold mountain streams. Years later, after I was an adult and would come home to the homestead, Dad would be up at sunrise, down at Alkali creek catching fresh trout. By the time my family was getting up for the day he was frying up the fish. He would set back and enjoy watching me, as with great delight, I would enjoy my favorite kind of breakfast. But I think even to this day, the most delicious trout I ever ate was setting around the campfire with Billy listening to his scary stories.

I have had the privilege of knowing earthly shepherds who have been faithful to care for their flocks of sheep, how much more does the Great Shepherd care for the individual sheep in the form of you and me? Two portions of scripture that I read on a regular basis are chapters 37 and 51 of the Psalms.

Trust in the Lord and do good;
dwell in the land and enjoy safe pasture.
Take delight in the Lord, and he will give you
the desires of your heart. Psalm 37:3 & 4 NIV

Create in me a pure heart, O God, and renew
a steadfast spirit within me.
Do not cast me from your presence or take
your Holy Spirit from me. Restore to me the
joy of your salvation and grant me a willing spirit,
to sustain me. Psalm 51:10 & 12 NIV

It is God's desire that all of mankind would be fed in pastures of His righteousness and goodness. We have been given a free will to choose this life of rich abundance. The reason I have such a love for these passages of scripture is because of my own personal experiences throughout my own life when I would ask this Shepherd of Heaven to keep my heart tender and pliable in his hands.

As each individual walks his or her personal journey through this life, heartache and trouble will come along side at some point. This is a verse I keep close by.

"I will never leave you or forsake you."
Hebrews 13:5 NKJV

This is vital to you and I in the times we are living. The personal commitment of taking the time to walk in spiritual pastures comes back to sustain us in the hard times. Having the insight to know that we have been cared for through the hardships by this faithful God is what brings the joy and peace so that we do find ourselves desiring to worship and praise the God of this universe.

I could pen many scriptures related to the Great Shepherd's desire to provide green pastures for his sheep, but I will settle for two.

"Then we your people, the sheep of your pasture, will praise you forever; from generation to generation we will recount your praise.
Psalm 79:13 NIV
Come, let us bow down in worship, let us kneel before the Lord our Maker; for he is our God and we are the people of his pasture the flock under his care." Psalm 95:6 & 7 NIV

It says that the very hairs of our head are numbered. How God loves the deepest part of man, where he is not even aware, is beyond my comprehension.

When I interviewed Teddy about how she fed and cared for the lambs, she spoke from a lifetime of knowledge and dedication to that calling she and Ronnie have given their lives for. I can pen the words from the transcript of Teddy's interview, but the emotion and compassion she possessed as she spoke could only be experienced in its entirety setting there at the dining room table on that blustery March afternoon.

"You asked me to talk about one of my very favorite topics and that is raising bum lambs. The more I am around sheep, it is apparent to me that this is one of my callings from God; to be a shepherdess and care for his kids, his creatures. It is so rewarding to take those baby lambs when their mama doesn't want them and love them and care for them and watch them grow. God has created all those creatures and so it brings me great pleasure.

We start off our baby lambs, usually called bum, but you can call them an orphan. In the sheep world we usually call them bum lambs.

They are actually an orphan lamb because the mother cannot feed the lamb. We have two types of lambs we call bums. One group of lambs is fed a supplement, as the mother ewe will not have enough milk because she has triplets or one side of the udder is no longer functioning so we have to supplement milk for the lamb. These lambs usually stay with their mother. The first nineteen days these lambs will be fed three times a day, or twice a day, depending upon how much they are getting from their mother. We watch them closely to see how they are doing and judge accordingly. These lambs are fed until they are about forty-seven days of age. By this time the lamb can consume enough roughage in order to maintain and grow and really gain and do well. Before that time their stomach isn't large enough to consume enough calories and nutrients.

The other set of bum lambs are true orphans. They are taken from their mother for some reason. Sometimes we have a ewe that does not like her baby and so consequently she will be very mean with the lamb. If we leave the baby with her she will butt it and could break the lamb's ribs. We have had to rescue some lambs with broken legs, such as Susie that we will tell you about. We had one ewe that lay on her lambs. We thought we had put too much straw in the pen, so we gave her another lamb, and she laid on that lamb too. She just didn't like the baby lambs at all, so she is no longer on the Jones farm.

Sometimes a ewe will die and we will try and work that lamb onto another ewe. In four or five days she usually takes the lamb, but if she butts the lamb around we have to take it, and it will become a bum lamb. Some years we have an abundance of triplets, and because of space at least one of those lambs will become a bum.

In the first two days, I have to make sure that the bums without any of the mother's milk are getting colostrum. We get this colostrum milk from the dairy. This first milk from the ewe or from the diary is really important. If these lambs don't get enough colostrum they will look like they are doing well and all of a sudden they will get sick and die.

We have documented this so we have learned through the years how vital the colostrum is in those first few days. It starts forming the antibodies that help to defend and fight off the diseases that the lamb might get.

So the first two days I feed the bum lambs colostrum three times a day. After that, I mix the colostrum half-and-half with lamb replacement milk. A ewe's milk is high in fat content versus calf milk replacement, so it is important that we use the lamb replacement.

When I have a lot of bum lambs, I use a wooden board with eight holes for the milk bottles. I try to group the lambs by age and size. We feed each lamb ten ounces of milk per feeding. For the first nineteen days, we feed the bum lambs three times a day. This would be around the clock, as they are very much like a newborn baby.

In each lamb pen is a feeder with lamb pellets that contain about nineteen percent protein. It is dense in vitamins and minerals to give the lambs a good start. It is very important to keep fresh water in the pens for the lambs all the time.

We keep the lambs in groups of eight, so they can get around the feeders easily. They start forming friendships. Sheep are social animals and if you take one of the lambs out, it will cry and cry because you have separated it from its friends. After we have moved the lambs from these small pens, we keep the groups of eight together because they have bonded to each other. Sheep are creatures of habit, and they like to be in familiar surroundings.

After the nineteenth to the twenty-third day we observe the lambs closely. This is the period of time when they start to consume a good deal of dry feed and we are trying to drop back from the thirty ounces of milk a day to twenty. During this time is when the lambs will bloat as the proportions of milk and feed are not balanced in the lamb. We give the lambs bloat guard starting around the tenth day, but we still have to watch them closely. Bloating causes gas to build up in the lamb's stomach. The stomach will blow up like a balloon and it can get so full, that the gas will rupture the diaphragm. The lamb will not be able to breath, and it will die. This can happen in a matter of just a few hours. That is why it so critical to watch these lambs very closely.

If we can discover the bloating early, we will give the lamb milk of magnesia. If this doesn't relieve the pressure, the last resort is to stick the lamb's stomach with a long needle to release the pressure of the gas so it won't build up any more. This is a problem we have to deal with, as we can lose a lamb very quickly.

Another problem we have with baby lambs is pneumonia. The bums suck fast on the bottle, and the milk can go down into the lamb's windpipe. If they can't cough up the milk, it will go down into their lungs and cause them to have chronic pneumonia.

The third thing we have to be careful of is scours. This type of diarrhea in the lamb will cause it to become dehydrated very quickly and die. These are the three main killers of our bum lambs, so we watch them very carefully.

As you can see from this very brief description, these bum lambs require a great deal of work and close observation. It is rewarding because they are just like children. They are your babies and you know without your care they would end up in the trash can.

We call them our trash can babies. If we didn't care for them, love them, feed them and doctor them that is where they would end up.

It is rewarding, because these little bum lambs become bonded to their caregiver. They know your voice. When you go out and call, "Here Lamby, lamby, lamby," they just come running. Even after they become grown ewes, and have their baby lambs, they are not afraid. They will come right up and nuzzle you. They know who you are. Ronnie says, "You've got to love them. If you don't love them, then don't raise sheep." Sheep can lie down and die so easily, so they need to be cared for and loved."

Once again as I read the description Teddy spoke of in her interview, there were pictures in my mind, so clearly remembered, of not only what she said, but how she truly loved those little bum lambs. How it brings to mind, the Heavenly Shepherd who desires to care for each of us in such a tender way. It is His desire to feed us with heavenly manna. Each of us was in his mind, before this world was created. How sad, that we often do not take the time to allow Him to feed us with spiritual food that will make us strong, and at peace.

Our society has become very aware of the need for good nutrition, healthy diet, need for organic foods, and so on. The statement, "You are what you eat," has a good deal of research data to back it up.

I remember a scripture I used to read in Sunday School when I was a young child. After all these years, I think about the parable of the sower planting seed, and check my mind and heart on a regular basis.

A farmer went out to sow his seed. As he was scattering the seed, some fell along the path; it was trampled on, and the birds ate it up. Some fell on rocky ground, and when it came up, the plants withered because they had no moisture. Other seed fell among thorns, which grew up with it and choked the plants. Still other seed fell on good soil. It came up and yielded a crop, a hundred times more than was sown. Luke 8:5-8 NIV

We are admonished to read the Bible. It is God's inspired word. I do not understand how it can be so life changing to make it a regular habit to read and study the Bible. I have found time and again, that at just the moment I need an answer or hope in a situation, those verses that are in my mind and spirit will come into clear focus like a road map.

Another source of inspiration is to read about saints who have gone before us. Many of them lived through crucibles of life's hardships, yet God was faithful to care for them and this brings me courage. To realize that Jesus Christ loves each of us in such a unique and precious way fills my life with much joy.

CHAPTER 4
LEADS BY STILLWATERS

　　If I would use words to describe myself, one of the trains of thought that would be at the top of the list is that I am a dreamer. I see life with a cup half full or better brimming over, as the creativity that takes many forms brings me pure joy. Even as a young girl I would draw house plans. I was careful to place the large windows so that I would be sure and see the sunrise and sunset. As a girl riding out in the foothills of the rugged mountains, I would see sunsets that were magnificent in those Wyoming clear blue skies.

　　The windows in my home in Shell, Wyoming had been designed to catch the eastern and western skies of beauty. During those years I lived in the apartment with a southern exposure looking out on my garden in the forest, I could not see either the sunrise or sunset so I drew a great deal of house plans.

I wanted to share this picture of my everyday friends, the sand cranes near the water's edge. I had moved into my lake cottage last winter. One of those desires of this dreamer was to someday live next to a lake. There are not adequate words to describe the joy I had as I would look out on the frozen waters knowing that in just a few months I would be out swimming in the lake. That first month I worked long hours getting my cottage in order.

I remember well February 11, 2021. I came down with Covid. My family worried about me being in the cottage but they checked on me daily and brought those things I needed. I knew I was gravely ill. I just could not breathe and the headaches lasted for weeks. Since I had experienced a concussion a few years earlier, I knew I needed to be very quiet and not tax my brain. I described it as if my brain was in a muddle, as I could not think or remember anything but for a short time. I tried not to listen to the news as I would hear of so many elderly dying alone in nursing homes away from family. I would manage to make it out to the living room, open the blinds and look out on the lake as this would seem to bring a solace to my soul.

I had written the grief manuscript, "Timmy the Timid, Timmy the Tender, Tools for Coping with Grief," a few years earlier after my beloved Yorky pet had died.

I slowly began to regain my strength and knew I needed to get the grief book published, hoping I could bring hope and courage to others suffering from the pandemic.

It was a very slow process and also frustrating as I would have to limit the writing each day. One morning after the manuscript had gone to the publisher I strolled out very early as the sunrise was coming up over the lake. My everyday sand crane friends walked all around me as I sat there in my lawn chair at the water's edge. The morning mist was rising up over the lake and gave an essence of God's glory.

That morning I just wept for joy, as I was so grateful the book was finished and that I had survived from a time I was so very ill.

Now I could come into summer looking out on a dream I had carried with me for most of my life.

As long as I can remember I have had a fascination with water. I will share a few of my own experiences. Before those personal encounters with water I want to share a portion of the interview with Ronnie and Teddy once again.

The importance of still waters and green pastures is contained in verse 2 of the 23rd Psalm. Teddy and Ronnie both expressed the need for nutritious food, as well as a steady supply of fresh water.

I asked Ronnie to explain the significance of the portion of the verse, "Leads by still waters." He replied, "Sheep require a considerable amount of water to help out with digestion and with body temperature regulation. Still water gives the sheep a better chance to get a good drink. It is more difficult for sheep when the water is fast moving. It is more peaceful for them to go up and get a drink if the water isn't splashing in their face. Sheep don't like to have water thrown in their face, just like you or I wouldn't want water splashed in our face.

Sheep also have a sense that they don't want to get down in the water, as it drags them down. When the wool gets wet it becomes very heavy, so it can be a danger to get up and out of the water."

During those days we spent in the lambing sheds, Nathan would be making his rounds on a regular time schedule checking all the pens to assure the sheep had a steady supply of fresh water.

Wyoming will always have a special place in my heart. It can be described as high desert so there are not many lakes, but the Rocky Mountains are majestic. On the other hand, Michigan is lush and green with lakes sprinkled all over the state including several of the great lakes.

Days to Remember at Lake Michigan

The winter months can be brutal, so those of us who live in Michigan want to make the very most of those summer days as they move by much too quickly. My grandchildren are now young adults, but in those growing up years we made a huge effort to go to Lake

Michigan several times in the summer. One of our favorite places to visit was Van Buren state park. As we would drive up to the gate of the park we all looked for the flag that would indicate how the waves were that day. Secretly, as a grandmother, I always hoped for green. Now the grandsons would be full of joy if it was red. Although there were days, it was too dangerous to swim. The family has many wonderful memories of sharing Michigan's beautiful water. I will always be grateful that we just stopped all the busy schedules and went swimming for the day.

Those times we spent at Lake Michigan with the grand children were filled with much laughter, quiet moments of sharing our lives of living, but also when the heartaches would come, it seems swimming out together to the sand bar and crying together would make the sorrow manageable, such as the summer my children's father past away.

I always was delighted to hear Shana tell of her special needs students she cared for as a nurse. Just to see her compassion and love for those children so challenged with life threatening illnesses made me so proud I am her Mom. I have told her many times, she is as an angel sent to those families.

One of those memories comes to mind. I can't remember the color of the flag that day but I am sure it was not green. Shana and the kids headed for the waves. She had found a sand bar a distance out. I could see her as the waves would turn her over. Her exuberant laughter at the fun of the challenging waves was like music to my ears. Seeing the smiles and hearing the laughter of grandchildren at the beach has to be one of life's most special pleasures.

It was my turn to enjoy the waves. The grandsons exclaimed in unison, "Oh Grandma are you coming in?"

Gabe, Perry and Kam Lewis with Grandma at Lake Michigan

The water was colder this time. I inched out to about waist deep. A big wave caught me, off came my plastic flip-flop type shoes, upending, I went down to the bottom, trying to right myself. The waves came again with a smashing force. This wasn't fun! I gulped and took in the lake water. The lake floor was covered with rocks. My feet are very tender, so it was hard to stand up. As I spit up water and called for the kids to grab my shoes I looked over to see a couple standing nearby watching this little old grandma. By the looks on their faces, I realized they thought I was in trouble. I was embarrassed to hear them say, "Should we go help that old woman?" I sheepishly drug myself out of the water as the boys ran and collected my shoes.

What happened to this lover of the sea? Seasons of life have a way of changing us. There was no way I was going to complain and put a damper on the exuberant laughter of my family. I realized I needed more substantial shoes if I were to tangle again with the waves, so I found myself very content as I walked along the wet sand at the edge of the waves on shore. For the rest of the day I counted the heads of all four members of my family like an eagle on her perch, like a watchmen on the tower so to speak.

As we raise our children, the love we have for them is overwhelming at times. But when we grow into the grand parenting years, the love takes on a quality of seasoning from a lifetime of loving and experience.

I will now bring back my first memory of the mighty waves of the Pacific Ocean. My parents took us to San Diego to visit my mother's cousin Imogene and her family. They lived a few blocks from the ocean shore. I had to be watched carefully as I would run without abandon right out into the waves. From that point on I had a fascination for the ocean. The sand, the saltwater taste, the smells of ocean breezes, the call of seagulls all engulfed me into a world of fantasy and joy.

Cannon Beach, Oregon has to be one of the most beautiful places on this earth in my estimation. Many years ago while working on research I spent six weeks there in a small bungalow. I had a view of the ocean at my window as I spent the daylight hours writing on my homestead manuscript. It was the middle of October, so the evenings were cool. Every evening I would walk down to the beach with Timmy, my Yorky type dog.

I would wear an old hat, sleeveless shirt and walking shorts. I liked to run along right at the break of the water in the wet sand. Timmy would run off chasing seagulls, never with a chance of catching them. By the time I would be out of breath, my lips would be blue and my feet would be icy cold. It wasn't long before I was having some respiratory problems and a low grade fever. I was so mesmerized with the beauty of the sun setting over the water, that only later I would reflect on others walking along the sea shore as well. They were dressed with warm jackets, hats, and rubber knee boots.

The days grew too short during that brief period of enjoying the sea. Poems were written describing the deep felt sadness of leaving that northern seashore.

BEACHCOMBER

Here they come one by one, some in twos, once in a while a group of three talking and enjoying each other in this brief week-end excursion to the beach.
I quietly walk here on the water's edge with my small Yorky, his small legs running smiling as he goes. He loves the sand,
but seems to have an innate
respect for the ocean waves.
We beachcombers have an instinctive
respect for one another.
This ocean coastline is the solace place,
the spiritual sanctuary for the tired weary soul in a
world of high tech,
daily demands, and global pursuits.
I know in my heart, my time here on this vast ocean sand,
walking barefoot,
with the crashing waves always the focal point in view,
will come to an end too shortly.
And so I have moments of grief of my departure, even now.
How long have I carried this dream of setting on the warm sand,
breathing in the
Brisk morning air, filled with mist, and smell the soul cleansing

fragrance of salt water?
Passerby, you walk so quietly there.
Are you locked away also with your
creative inner thoughts of a rejuvenated spirit and soul.
Lovers in the distance, you walk together hand in hand.
Some of you so young, others walking with cane,
helping each other in your slow and stumbling gate.
Are you seizing the moment, letting by-gones pass away into the
vast ocean's expanse?
Loving each other, cherishing the moments that
will soon be gone.
I turn away giving you the privacy you deserve.
Walking on I pause, standing very still a few moments watching the
magnificent white waves
of foam silhouetted against turquoise water, at the base of
royal blue sky that reaches up into eternity.
Kindred spirit of the sea walking there so quietly, my heart blesses
you as you step so lightly, allowing my tears to come uninterrupted as
the inner voice within me is so over whelmed by the thoughts and
phrases coming so rapidly,
I at times would seem to be swept into the
depths of sorrow, and then rapidly be thrust up into the
greatest exaltation of soul.
I soon will take pen in hand and write,
but for a time of reprieve, I will again begin my stroll
along the beach with other lovers of the sea.
Patricia, 9-28-00

When viewing the Pacific Ocean at low tide on a calm day, it is hard to fathom that this same body of water was where one of the deadliest natural disasters occurred in December of 2004. The Tsunami which struck eleven countries with one hundred foot waves in less than ten minutes was responsible for over 225,000 deaths. The human suffering from this natural disaster cannot be measured. Many people saw family members swept away by the mighty waves and there was nothing they could do to save them.

The beauty and comfort of water, whether it be on a mountain stream or ocean coast, has been a focal point for many persons, as they will build homes right out on the sand, or near the falling stream over craggy rocks. Always in the back of the minds of individuals is the reality that this small body of water could become a flood of huge proportion with the right amount of snow runoff in the high mountains. The smooth and placid ocean shore has the possibility of turning into a catastrophic hurricane.

Some years ago our nation witnessed the destruction of many hurricanes. The nation came to realize in small proportion the magnitude of Hurricane Ike. There was a mandatory evacuation up and down the seacoast and yet many thought they could ride out the storm.

Life has it's times of pleasure, peace and much joy and then are those times that it seems a flood has come and wiped away every dream and voice of laughter to be heard.

When my oldest grandson Eric was five and John was three, they came with their father to meet me in Buffalo, New York where I had been attending a "Creative Problem Solving Institute." It had been an incredible experience for me to have the opportunity of spending a week at this conference, but also exhausting. The training was over, everyone was departing, and I sat waiting for Craig, anxious that he would be able to find me. The whole family had planned to come, but Sandy had to stay home with Elizabeth, as she had gotten sick in the night. When I saw him coming up the walk carrying Anna, with two young boys in tow, I wanted to cry with joy, it was so good to see my broad shouldered son with a stocky build. We loaded up the children and headed off to Niagara Falls.

We first went to view the lower falls which were nothing short of spectacular. What resonates in my mind as I bring that memory back into focus were the upper falls. Anna was in a stroller and I had both boys hands clutched firmly in mine. As we approached the upper falls, the water was flowing smoothly before it crested over the top of boulders. The power of the water was so great it seemed as if we were standing on top of the current as it moved quickly by. We were protected by a security fence, but just the thought of one of my grandchildren falling in those fast moving waters brought a dread to my mind.

If it were possible to set at a safe point and watch the Tsunami that swept across the Pacific Ocean one would have some grasp of the mighty power water can have. Or if there was a platform one could stand on right in front of the waters of the Niagara before she makes her mighty plunge downward, holding out hands with palms up to push back the volume of water, could we understand the power of this magnificent waterfall?

Not only is water a thing of power that can bring great destruction, but it is vital to human existence. The human frame can go much longer without food than water. Dehydration is a word I respect, after an experience I once had. I found myself being rushed to a hospital in Cebu, Philippines after a long night of sickness. Before that morning, I had never realized how quickly one could become so dangerously ill in such a short time. I recovered but the experience left me weakened for a period of time.

I always get uncomfortable when watching a movie, where the actors are lost out in a desert, all water is gone, and they are disoriented as to where the water hole is. I want to get up and go get a drink of water.

During my teens, one of the summer excursions every year was to take a group of 4-H friends up to the top of Heart Mountain, which looked to the east of our farming community. About ten of us of would load up in the back of the pick-up truck and my brother Mike would be the driver. I am relieved as I watch my grown children being so careful to strap their children into car seats today. I shudder when I think of some of our trips up the mountains in those teen years back in the fifties.

On one such trip, each of us was carrying part of the picnic which was to be eaten at the base of the rocky ledge at the top. This was no small climb on that hot summer day in August. I don't remember who was to blame, but the person carrying the water jug, dropped it on a big rock and broke it. This was early on, so we climbed most of the way without water. When we finally got to the top, we sat down under a tree for shade and tried to eat the sandwiches. They were hard to choke down. Why I remember the frosting, I haven't a clue, but someone had brought an angel food cake with orange frosting. As I looked at it, I was reminded of the hot sun up above. We didn't want to be rude, so we all ate a piece. It was a hot grumpy group of teen-agers that came down off of Heart Mountain that afternoon.

Many years have passed and I trust I am a bit wiser. When I drive through the parkways, with all of the running paths, I see young people all equipped with their thermoses attached to belts. There is an awareness of the need for a constant supply of water.

My parents were fishermen, so if Daddy had a pause in irrigation, we would head up to the North Fork to fish in the evening. It was not uncommon to drink out of a creek or dip a metal cup down into the river. One always hoped that a dead animal was not lying in the creek around the hillside out of sight.

Life has changed, as the concern of water contamination is something to be contended with. Bottled water has become a common commodity in homes today. How I would have enjoyed a bottle of water stuck in my back pocket the day I ate the angel food cake with orange frosting.

I lived in Shell during most of the time I worked with UW Extension Service. During that time there was a seven year drought. The Extension Agriculture agent worked closely with ranchers and farmers and also my family was farming in the Powell area, so the seven year drought was something I was very aware of. It was sad to drive through Wyoming, and see it dry up. After a few years, because of such a shortage of water, crops were plowed up, or not even planted. Summer ranges were diminished for summer grazing. In an arid land like Wyoming, it would be foolish to waste water. The land where my home was situated had water rights. I was always very careful when I watered my trees that I used only what was needed.

Later in the summer, the water supply would run out, which became difficult for everyone living in that area. Water is vital for survival.

In a spiritual sense Jesus speaks of thirst and living water in relation to God's spirit dwelling within man.

"Jesus stood and said in a loud voice,
"If anyone is thirsty, let him come to me and drink.
Whoever believes in me, as the Scripture has said, streams
of living water will flow from within him." John 7:37 NIV

Each of the gospels relates the incident when Jesus had been ministering to the throngs of people, evening was setting in and he was weary. It was time to go to another location. He and the disciples got into a boat and headed across a great expanse of water. In his weariness, Jesus went to the stern of the boat and fell into a deep sleep. A furious squall developed and waves were about to sink the boat. The disciples were terrified that they would drown.

"The disciples woke him and said to him,
"Teacher, don't you care if we drown?"
He got up, rebuked the wind and said to the waves.
"Quiet! Be still!" Then the wind died down and it was completely calm. He said to his disciples. "Why are you so afraid? Do you still have no faith?" Mark 4:38-40 NIV

The Shepherd of Heaven walks so closely and yet there is a responsibility for each individual to have the discipline to feed on green pastures of God's goodness.

Also to allow the Spirit of God to run as a fresh stream through one's life, as described in scripture, will sustain us when the difficult times come. I am reminded of the verse:

When the enemy comes in like a flood,
The Spirit of the Lord
will lift up a standard against him. Isaiah 59:19 NKJV

How many times have these words spoken in Isaiah brought me new courage to keep on this journey I have been on since a young child, like sands of the sea, I cannot count them.

CHAPTER 5

HE RESTORES MY SOUL

A short phrase found in the context of one of most well loved chapters in the Bible, the 23rd Psalm, "He restores my soul," has resonated meaning to countless individuals down through the ages.

The society we live into today wants a quick fix for the melancholy that comes with heartache and loss. One would only need thumb through a magazine off the shelf, and glance at advertisements for just about any kind of product. Do we see downcast faces, agonizing over losses? Hardly, smiles and greetings of the good life full of bliss, with no cares for tomorrow greet us, page after page.

The real picture of life does have those days that we could describe as downcast. The psalmist David gives us a picture of the sadness and the distress that follows, "Why so disturbed within me?" This was not a constant condition for David, as the verses presiding this lamenting question, describes him as going with the multitude into the house of God with joy and praise. And in the second part of this verse, we see that David had discovered how to handle his times of discouragement and how his strength would be renewed.

"Put your hope in God, for I will yet praise him, my Savior and my God." Psalm 42:5 NIV

Looking back over a time in my life that seems but a long ago memory in many ways, was a pivotal point in my own personal destiny. Our family had come through a tragedy which had affected each of us. The grief I felt was unrelentless as it seemed one wave of crying would be met with another. And than there were times I couldn't cry. During those days I poured myself into my work, driving myself to the point of exhaustion. The human frame does not thrive under this kind of pressure. I found myself being rushed to a hospital to be operated on for a ruptured disk in my lower back. The surgeon had reassured me that I would be just like new. What he failed to mention is that I would not be able to work for months and the pain after surgery would be worse than before.

I called my brother Mike, and asked if I could borrow a recliner chair that was in vacation trailer, parked out in the back of Mom's home. I wasn't going to be able to set up in a chair for some time. He of course said "Yes." I stayed with my mother for a few days after surgery, but the mountain range in view just outside my living room window was like a healing balm I needed to recover. A friend loaded up the chair and took me home to Shell. I lived very simply, could not drive, but as I lay in the recliner looking out at the clouds up over the mountain horizon holding my little dog in my lap, the Shepherd of Heaven came very close along side giving me hope that would soon turn into a surprise that I would never have expected.

After my children were raised I returned to Wyoming, the place of my childhood. I took a position with the University of Wyoming Cooperative Extension Service. The county where I was placed was near the Big Horn Mountains. I found a lovely home at the base of Shell canyon. From the picture windows and wrap around deck of my home, I had a breathtaking panoramic view of the lower mountains. I made a point of watching the eastern horizon over the tops of the purple mountains for the sunrises in the morning, and would finish the evening watching the radiant sunsets to the west.

The first day of the rest of my life

The day that is vivid in my mind, is the day I began to write. I had been alone at home for several weeks recovering from the back surgery. It was a cold day in March, with heavy snow falling all day. I could not sit up, so I was lying in a recliner looking out over the distance, studying the jagged outlines of rocks of the mountain landscape being covered with a blanket of snow. My heart was sad, and I was feeling overwhelmed with pain. As I sat there I was swept with an urgency to write. This was a surprise to me, as writing had always been difficult. I managed to get out of the recliner and go find a tablet. As I lay back down, I took a pen in hand and thus began a new chapter in my life. I wrote one page after another and would then read what I had actually put down.

Those first writings have been tucked away in a safe place. To have the courage to be able to pen those sorrows buried so deep inside was the beginning of inner healing for me. I put dates on each poem, later being very thankful, as I could see by the content as time passed my writing began to change. I came to an awareness that in the melancholy times I could draw strength and reflection that would be translated on the pages as hope and faith for the future. Those were not wasted days, as I recognized a sharper keenness to my surroundings, and insight into the suffering of others.

My own story can be described as a mirror reflection of others who find themselves in life's tragedies and call out to the Great Shepherd. How God takes the hard places and turns them around to build character in the heart of man is a constant reminder to me of his majesty and greatness.

At this point in my journey, when people ask me my view of life, I say with a chuckle, "I am going to be happy if it kills me." I was born with a laugh that seems to consume me, and draw others in as well. For a period of time, I didn't laugh very much. As I reflect back on the harder times of my own life, I find it interesting, those words that others spoke to me, that gave me the determination of a bulldog, to grow, regardless of the situation.

I would fly back to Michigan for the holidays, usually finishing up a quilt or French heirloom dresses for the grandaughters. My children always had a list of their favorite foods they remembered from childhood. I suppose this shows my homestead roots. When my own children were growing up, I wanted them to have vivid memories of home. I would try to plan to have things coming out of the oven just as the family stepped into the house from busy school activities and work schedules. Home made bread, cherry pie, and on and on the list would go. And they did remember. So I would get my list upon arrival. And of course, being Mom, I tried to squeeze in as much as possilbe. I do believe the chicken and noodles were always the favorite.

A Christmas holiday that was a highlight was the year Reagan was born in November. When I walked into Craig's home and saw that baby, it was like Craig had come back in the form of baby. John was only eight, but he was silly about that baby. He would carry him around, feed him, and he wanted to make sure all of Reagan's needs were met. He has his mother's fair skin, but his face is like looking at Craig. He has a sense of humor that just makes me smile. He gets so tickled as he watches cartoons and it is just delightful.

I always had at least one stop on my flight back to Wyoming, but while on the plane, I would have a book in hand, snoring all the way. Early on in my time with the university, after one of the holidays with the family, something was said that gave me the determination to get on with life. It had been an enjoyable time with the family. I had enjoyed the grandchildren, laughed a lot at Craigs' nonesense jokes, went to funny late night movies with Rachel and Sandy, and just loved being with the family. Sandy later told me what Craig had said after I had left. "Now that is how I remember my Mom!" Wow! I thought a great deal about that comment.

Those times of restoration are vital in one's growth, but there is a point of learning and gleaning, and then getting on with life. Life is a choice. We can choose to be happy or miserable. Unfortuently for those who enjoy their misery, they tend to dump it on to everyone else they come close to.

The 23rd Psalm relates to this Shepherd of Heaven who cares for the individual person, as depicted in the care over a lamb. How much more does he care for all the affairs of man?

For many years I taught a class entitled, "Creative Parenting." I would explain that when the children leave the nest, they have the right to live their own lives. But the fact of the matter is that we will always be the parent and we will always love our children even after they are grown. I have come to the conclusion that maybe the best gift we can give our grown children, is just be a good listener, love the granchildren, show up for the athletic events, give a word of advise, only when it is asked for, celebrate life with the family, share a lot of laughter and enjoy the simple things in life like chicken and noodles.

Sandy and Patricia Booher spending the afternoon at Meckley's apple orchard.

I have often thanked God for my dauhter-in-law Sandy. I remember well the college graduation day when both Sandy and Craig received their teaching degrees. She and I have had many delightful conversations about our love for children. We both realize that to have such a friendship and have those times of praying together is priceless.

God made this human frame of ours. He knew there would be times of sorrow, times when our spirit would need to be restored. Some of the greatest hymns ever written came from a broken hearted saint, who could hear the melody and words more clearly as they walked their own personal journey with this Shepherd of Heaven. I remember well my dear friend Mary Ellen Fraser playing such a song on her violen which I had always cherished. The melody, combined with the words penned have always been a source of comfort. I was grateful to the McClaflin family when this particular hymn was chosen for our father's funeral.

As one pauses to understand the circumstances surrounding the words, it only enhances the depth of passion mingled with sorrow that brought this beloved hymn to the world. Horatio Spafford, a wealthy businessman, lost his fortune due to the Chicago Fire in October of 1871. His family was crossing the Atlantic shortly after this disaster. The ship they were traveling on collided with another ship. Stafford's four daughters were lost at sea. His wife Anna sent him a telegram, with the crushing words; "Saved alone."

Stafford was traveling across the Atlantic weeks later, and as he passed the place where his daughters were drowned, the words of this song came to him. The Heavenly Shepherd speaks to us by his Holy Spirit. I will penn but a few of the lines of this beautiful hymn.

"It Is Well With My Soul"

But, Lord, 'tis for Thee, for Thy coming we wait,

The sky, not the grave, is our goal;

Oh trump of the angel! Oh voice of the Lord!

Blessed hope, blessed rest of my soul!

Is is well, with my soul, It is well, with my soul,

It is well, it is well, with my soul.

And Lord, haste the day when my faith shall be sight,

The clouds be rolled back as a scroll;

The trump shall resound, and the Lord shall descend,

Even so, it is well with my soul.

The human frame does not have a built in button that can be pushed for patience. When one comes to those pauses in life when time is required to restore that inner person, it is hard to wait. Whether restoration is required because of grief, a major life change, a sinful act, or an injustice, time is required. Everyone has a story.

"You just don't know how I have suffered?" How easy it is to fall into the pit of self-pity, which only increases the time for healing. It doesn't take long, as we look around to find someone else whose trials are far worse than our own.

Psalm 23 could be a road map for the entire life span. I am grateful for the brief verse, "He restores my soul," indicating there will times we need the reassurance of this shepherd that he can take those broken and bruised places of our lives, and bring us to a heightened level of awareness and growth. Most likely this growth will not come without some pain, whether physical, emotional, or a combination of both.

Those times of reflection when one walks through periods of restoring of spirit are enhanced with the five senses. Later we can remember a particular place, what season of the year it was. A particular song or fragrance can bring back a sorrow or memory long buried or forgotten. As I pen the words to the page today, my mind goes back to a place I would like to be as I write this chapter. It was a private place where I could set on a large boulder, fly pole in hand, and hear the late summer sounds of water running down a steep mountain cliff. I often drove up to the Shell falls when the afternoon heat became too heavy, but this place was more private. There was a pull out area where I could park my car. It only took me five minutes to drive there from my house.

On days I had the luxury of being home, there were always chores to be done. But just to slip away to this private place under the bridge would restore my spirit in such a way that I would be rejuvenated.

The heavy wooden cattle bridge that had been constructed many years ago had been used for bands of sheep and herds of cattle to cross over Shell creek in order to reach the path that led up into the Big Horn Mountain range used for summer pasture

There was a pull off area where I could park my car next to the bridge. Cars would whip by just coming down from the switch backs on the west side of the mountain. Near the underbrush there was a deer trail where I could make my way down to the water.

The cattle bridge in Shell, Canyon in Wyoming

Even in the late summer the water was cold and clear. I would nestle in the crevice of the large boulder and get out my fly pole. A friend had been very patient to give me lessons.

I enjoy watching fly fishermen out on the mountain streams. The movement of the orange fishing line making its silhouette of circles out over the water could be described as a symphony in motion. My casting would be decidedly more like circle around, stop, disconnect the hook from the tree branches, and then start the process all over again.

I don't think I ever caught a trout in those little pools at the base of Shell canyon. I spent more time studying the rock formations and enjoyed listening to the rustle of the leaves in the trees overhead that gave a protection of shade. From where I sat under the bridge, only the tops of the cars were visible as they sped by. It was a quiet sanctuary where I was at peace.

WOUNDS OF THE SOUL

On those days we are busy catching up on filing or writing or whatever in the home office, one of those annoying happenings is to have a paper cut. Although it is not that painful we know it will take a few days to heal. In this writing I will not be talking about those minor flesh wounds, but rather those very serious cuts into the flesh that will most likely leave a permanent scar.

I relate this snippet of story to the scripture that warns of those wounds that can even divide soul and spirit. That soulish part of man with all the emotions of humanity that each of us deal with could be placed in the category of wounds of the soul.

I remember a situation when I was in the eighth grade. It was harvest time and my father was out in the shop working on the combine. A large metal bar broke loose and hit the under part of his arm. If it had hit him in the head he would have died instantly. This was a very traumatic experience for our family as even as young as I was I knew he was seriously wounded.

What is amazing about this small Heart Mountain homestead community is when there is a sickness or injury all the farm neighbors rally around and bring their combines and harvest the crops. This is still a practice that goes on with those dear friends. The harvesting equipment can be seen way down the road.

It was such a serious break that my father was in the hospital for days. Not only were there bones broken but much damage was done to the nerves and muscles.

The cast created an open wound at the wrist which took a long time to heal. I was very young then, but now I understand how serious this flesh wound had become. This deep wound would prove to create a lasting scar and damage to my father's hand. The fingers drew up leaving his hand withered making it hard to do many of his tasks.

I was surprised later in life when my father told me he was embarrassed about his hand. That had never occurred to me, because he was my Daddy and I loved his hard working hands.

The Creator of this universe created within the human frame the ability to heal and replace. The flesh around the wound dries up and new skin begins to develop underneath the surface as the wound heals. It is very important to keep the open wound clean and undisturbed in the healing process. As the wound heals one is tempted to scratch but this only opens up the wound with the danger of introducing germs and infection which delays healing.

In this brief writing, I will be speaking of those wounds of the heart and soul. There are some wounds we receive that can relate to the paper cut in the skin. These wounds affect our emotions, feelings and relationships, but with time we manage to work through the process of healing and forgiving is an added bonus.

When I was a young girl, I often heard the phrase, "Sticks and stones may break my bones but words will never hurt me." It does not take very long walking out this journey called life to realize, that is far from the truth. For words spoken can never really be retrieved, but one must grapple with the pain of it all.

There is a type of wound that will heal, but a permanent scar will be imbedded in the soul and sometimes the wound is so deep it goes down into the spirit. I am speaking of those conditions that cannot be reversed such as the death of a child, divorce, loss of a parent and sometimes a cherished pet, death through violence and the list goes on.

It takes courage and a great deal of faith in some situations to walk on in life. One of the hardest statements to hear is the one, who seems clueless to the wounded soul. "Oh just get on with it, get over it." Well, if you are the one with the broken heart, you so much want to get on. Wow, the pain subsides and we think we are just fine and then something so insignificant, maybe an old song, or something else just hits you smack right between the eyes and the grief returns. Now with time if one has a brave heart there are tools we can learn for coping. At this point, I want to make it clear, I am not describing, the forever victim, who spends, not only their time, but anyone else who they can drag into their story of misery and woe.

The book of Hebrews found in the New Testament of the Bible is described as a book of faith. One of those scriptures I have often referred to as I exam my own heart in difficult and painful situations is as follows.

For the word of God is living and powerful, and sharper than any two-edged sword, piercing even to the division of soul and spirit, and of joints and marrow, and is a discerner of the thoughts and intents of the heart. Hebrews 4:12 NKJV

The spirit of a man will sustain him in sickness, but who can bear a broken spirit? Proverbs 18:14 NKJV

I am presently writing the second edition of a book on the 23rd Psalm. I have always found a place in my own life for the entire of book of Psalms as I relate to that young shepherd boy David as he moved among his flocks of sheep. I would call myself even now in my later years a shepherd girl. The beauty in the scriptures and knowing this Shepherd of Heaven is that he is the great healer of soul, body and spirit. He is the faithful friend and takes on the role of our father many times in our days of sorrow.

Seeing then that we have a great High Priest who has passed through the heavens, Jesus the Son of God, let us hold fast our confession. For we do not have a High Priest who cannot sympathize with our weaknesses, but was in all points tempted as we are, yet without sin. Let us therefore come boldly to the throne of grace that we may obtain mercy and find grace to help in time of need.

Hebrews 4:14 – 16 NKJV

One of my favorite research books on resiliency, is "Adversity Quotient" by Paul Stoltz, PhD. He defines how one handles adversity in three groups. I would categorize wounds of soul and spirit a challenge that each of us will face in this journey called life. The quitter just barely gets by and this is where the victim can find themselves. It is always someone else's fault. "No one has ever suffered as I have." The camper on the other hand has made it half way up the mountain and when the winds of adversity come along with the cold blast, they set up their tent and go no farther.

The picture of overcoming adversity is that one who chooses to be the climber. They see the top of the mountain in view and nothing will deter their journey. They can be heard to say; "Don't feel sorry for me that is a luxury I cannot afford." No matter how great the trial they are walking through, they know they can find someone else who is having a harder time and they just want to make a difference. This kind of faith and overcoming takes more courage than is contained in the human frame, so to be able to just humble one's heart and let the Shepherd of Heaven come and bring healing is a beautiful picture of redemption.

I will briefly speak of those wounds that can come within the family or even in a congregation of those we have called friend.

Fearfulness and trembling have come upon me,

For it is not an enemy who reproaches me;
Then I could bear it.

Nor is it one who hates me who has exalted himself against me;

Then I could hide from him.

But it was you, a man my equal,

My companion and my acquaintance.

We took sweet counsel together,

And walked to the house of God in the throng.

He has redeemed my soul in peace from the battle

that was against me,

Because they do not change,

Therefore they do not fear God.

He has put forth his hands against those who were at peace with him;

He has broken his covenant.

The words of his mouth were smoother than butter

But war was in his heart;

His words were softer than oil,

Yes they were drawn swords.

Cast your burden on the Lord

And He shall sustain you;

He shall never permit the righteous to be moved.

Psalm 55: 5 – 22 NKJV

    I have found in my own journey, I am what one would call a peace maker. I do not thrive in conflict. In fact I will go to great lengths to just bring peace to a situation. Oh yes, I have read Psalm 55 many times down through the years. Through much sorrow there have been those times I have had to recognize, the only way I can really choose to have peace and forgiveness is to rely on the Heavenly Shepherd's strength.. To take on another's troubles when they do not want to take responsibility only depletes me of energy and vision of what I have been assigned and that is to write these snippets of encouragement to those other climbers who have asked the Shepherd of Heaven to walk along side of them.

As I have walked my own journey there have been times I just could not understand "Why?" I just know that this Shepherd of Heaven is a God of justice. As we look around today, it seems the daily news is filled with much injustice. Coming from my homestead roots I often wonder is there any horse sense or it can be called common sense. What I have experienced countless times in those difficult situations, if I just take the time to be quiet and ask the Lord to sustain me and give me the grace, patience and forgiveness, he is always faithful. The Shepherd of Heaven is the great healer of all wounds and one day when we see him in Heaven what a beautiful time that will be.

Cast your burden on the LORD,
And He shall sustain you;
He shall never permit the righteous to be moved.

Psalm 55:22 NKJV

One of my tools of coping with the sadness, when it comes, is just to sit quietly and often the words of a poem or snippet of a story will seem to surface and as I begin to write the thoughts, then the calmness of my own spirit seems to return in a gentle way.

MOONLIGHT ON THE WATER

It is just before the dawn of morning when the world is silent and still. The lake has begun to be cast over with ice, but in the last few days the sunrays have made the waters move freely. But it is cold this morning and the black waters would bring danger to the careless swimmer. My soul and spirit take in this solemn quiet space of light that shimmers with an unearthly iridescent glow of beauty from the moon across the lake.

This is a morning of sorrow for me. Those deep desires of the heart of just wanting to give that kind word that goes unheeded brings a grief that is deep. I have traveled this narrow road in times past, and know there are those things I will not change and for that I weep.

And then as I stand looking deep into the light of the moon that will so quickly be gone over the horizon.

I remember so well that often in this journey called life, it is the darkest before the dawn.

In a short while I will again take hold of the faith in this master of the universe who has always been with me throughout my journey and I will sing of the glory he gives in the deepest times of sadness.

Patricia, December 20, 2021

Chapter 6

He Leads Me in the Paths of Righteousness

On this topic of righteousness, one would think that after a process of time, the integrity and truth of living a life in righteousness would be automatic. I have not found that to be true in my own life. In fact as the years roll by much too quickly now, daily I am drawn back to scripture and spending time in quiet solitude of prayer asking the Shepherd of Heaven to fashion my life after his.

In this chapter I have included short portions of life the way our community lived back in the early 50s. The Heart Mountain homestead community was a tight knit group of people who respected and worked together. It was a rugged way of life and even then, we felt like we were modern day pioneers. Even as very young children, we worked hard giving us a work ethic that would be a benefit to our society today.

FEED THE CHICKENS

In those early years on the homestead, every family member had a job. After coming home on the school bus, one of my chores was to feed the chickens. I didn't have a horse yet, so I had to get by with a long stick with a rope tied at the top to substitute for reins. I made trails out through the weeds and could entertain myself for a good deal of time in my fantasy world of being a cowgirl. One night it was almost dark when my Dad asked me if I had fed the chickens. Of course that was the last thing on my mind. I don't remember so much that he scolded me, but he did set me down and explain to me that the family was depending on me to do my part on this homestead. I never cared a great deal for those chickens because they would peck my hand when I gathered the eggs, but that night I began to have empathy for those chickens out in the barn. Later in life, when a situation would arise in which determination and loyalty was needed, I would hear myself say, "Just get up and go feed the chickens."

WWII

The Great War was over but not all the veterans came home to their families. I was almost two before I was introduced to my father. He had been a pilot with the WWII Army Air Corp. As a child, I always sensed a sadness that wasn't tangible but it was there. While he and his co-pilot were flying back to London at night from a mission the engine of the plane caught fire and most of the crew were lost in the bitter cold waters of the English Channel before rescue was possible. A small piece of my father's parachute was caught by the wind, so he was located just before he drowned. As the years quickly pass in my own life, I have wished many times that I would have asked him about his experience. It was a subject never broached with him. I did notice he never swam with the family. I heard him comment once, "I don't want to swim anymore, after my big dip."

When I was doing interviews with the homesteaders for the research project, I came to understand, that the veterans spoke very rarely with their families about the war. But they would talk with each other upon occasion. One summer afternoon I was visiting Lyle and Dorothy French, taping both of them as they told their family history. I had spent a good deal of time with them. The recorder had been turned off, and I was getting ready to walk out the door. Lyle began to talk about my Dad. He told me of a time he and my dad were staying together while attending a 4-H conference. It was late at night and they had returned to their motel room. Daddy sat on the side of the bed taking off his shoes. He began to tell of the night his plane went down in the English Channel, his voice cracking, as he mourned the loss of all those friends from so long ago. "I was one of the pilots flying the plane and I could not save my crew." Lyle came over next to me. "Pat, I just told him, Wallace, you've got to forgive yourself, it wasn't your fault."

I held on to the door knob of the outside door looking at Lyle. I was afraid I was going to break down right there and weep for my dad. I managed to keep my composure until I got into the car. I cried all the way home, knowing somehow, instinctively even as a child, there was a sadness about my father that he kept so deep inside of him.

Growing up in that community of war veterans, the children were given a sense of the greatness of this country. Seeing the American flag flying and hearing the national anthem brought a sense of responsibility.

In the Presidential election year of 1952, we still did not have electricity yet out in Heart Mountain community. One afternoon is still in my memory. Mike and I had come into the house after riding the school bus. Our living room was filled with neighbors listening to a battery operated radio. The election returns were coming in and there was great excitement as Eisenhower was going to be the next president. I was only in the second grade, so I couldn't understand all the issues and the whole process of elections and the differences between the Democrats and Republicans. What resonated in my young girl's mind were the awesome privileges we had and the reverence that was given to the President of the United States.

Elections for the President of this country roll around every four years. Seems in this age of the Internet and all the modern ways of mass communication, it only increases the times of being swamped with political strategies. Down inside most of us, we hope that just maybe this election year will be different. Honesty, integrity, concentrating on the vital issues that affect citizens of this great country will be the center focus. But alas, as the months approach the upcoming election in November and the finish line is in sight, we find the central focus changes into an ugly accusation of character. Which party can be the cleverest in this process of mental assassination of the opposing candidate? The ugliest part of this process is that we find ourselves getting caught up in the fight. Well-honed speeches can be so full of incorrect information that after a point we find that we are wondering what the truth really is. My father used to tell me, "If you can't say something good about someone it would be better to be quiet." Those words are burrowed deep into my heart, but I can't say that I always live up to the wisdom he imparted so long ago.

ELECTION YEAR

In my lifetime, I have followed many election years but I have to say that in the last few years it has become more cut-throat. Regardless of party affiliation, there have been nights I have just turned off the news, as I have been ashamed at what was being said.

Because of my son Craig's influence in having an innate understanding of the political scene, our family has a keen interest in the governmental process. On election night his telephone line is hot. Within our family, we jokingly say "We need a Craig Fix," when the election returns are coming in. If Craig's line is busy, then my phone starts ringing and I will hear an impatient voice on the other line, "I can't get a hold of Craig!"

One thing is sure; we love this country of ours. God Bless America! Our family likes to sing and break out in harmony when patriotic songs are being sung and often the feelings of respect for how this nation has been blessed will move us to tears.

Before I began to write this morning, I turned to the Bible passage, I Corinthians 13. I have made it a regular habit to read these verses and there are times I realize I fall short of the truth in the words laid down as a road map.

From the time my son Craig was a very young boy, it appeared he had a wisdom, I would describe as a universal knowledge of history. I was blessed the day he told me he wanted to be a history teacher, as I have cherished my own years of teaching. For thirty years Craig poured his wisdom into his high school and college students.

It was a sad day for Craig when he retired from teaching and couching, but there had always been that dream of having an Italian restaurant. There were many hurdles in planning a new company during the Covid lockdown, but now it is a reality.

The bonus in the difficult transition is he once again can meet with his countless students as they are so happy to see their history teacher, Mr. Booher. Craig was awarded the Michigan history teacher of the Year in 2007.

The 23rd Psalm relates to this Shepherd of Heaven who cares for the individual person, as depicted in the care over a lamb. How much more does he care for all the affairs of man?

Craig and his mother, Patricia Booher

I have often referred to this passage of scripture when praying for our nation, along with other countries of this world.

If my people, who are called by My name, will humble themselves, and pray and seek My face and turn from their wicked ways, then I will hear from heaven and will forgive their sin and will heal their land. 2 Chronicles 7: 14 NKJV

Coming into this season of my life, some refer to as the "Golden Years," I have come to the conclusion that one of the finest compliments that could be paid as an epitaph whether it is a man or woman, would be "That person was an individual of principle." Within the human frame is the desire to find such a genuine person, who truly has a servant's heart.

EAGLES EYESIGHT

Setting out on the deck looking out over the mountain range in Shell, an added bonus was when the eagles could be seen out on the horizon. The majestic wing span and beauty of these mighty birds was incredible to see at such close range. As they circled around the valley they could see small animals from a great distance. I watched my small Yorky with a sharp eye, as the thought of him becoming a meal for one of these powerful birds was more than I could imagine.

I have known persons who were terrified at the thought of flying in a plane... not me! I don't recall ever being anxious before a plane ride.

There have been times I have prayed when there was turbulence, or during a long overseas flight when the weariness set in. On flights when the weather was overcast, I always have gotten a certain thrill as the plane ascended up above the cloud mass. Remembering the speed that an eagle could elevate itself with its powerful wing spread up through the cumulus volumes of brilliant white would always invigorate my spirit. Flying high above the clouds, the eagle can look down through the haze to see a minute object. That brings to mind a favorite scripture:

And God Raised us up with Christ and seated us with him in the heavenly realms in Christ Jesus, in order that in the coming ages he might show the incomparable riches of his grace, expressed in his kindness to us in Christ Jesus. Ephesians 2.6 NIV

Just to know that we have been given a choice in this matter is incredible to me. This wonderful life of walking in the righteousness of God, which allows man to have the insight and wisdom of setting in those heavenly places with God, has been promised to those who walk with this Great Shepherd.

ALFRED CAWSTON

I think that I am most fortunate when I look back over my life and realize those persons who have invested so much in me. I attended Central Bible College in Springfield Missouri in 1964. There was a professor there who is vivid in my mind. He was only teaching for a year as a Missionary in Residents. He had founded the Southern Asia Bible College in 1951. He and his wife Elizabeth had been missionaries for thirty years. The impact of the work they did had been felt in many parts of the world. At the time I was a student so I didn't know much about this professor other than he inspired me with a Godly zeal that has always been with me. I took as many classes as I could that year with him.

There were several days when a time of prayer broke out with the students in the second semester. The power of God that swept over that campus came with prayer that started early and lasted way into the night. He was a key figure in leading that time of worship and prayer that was touched with a divine manifestation of God's glory. Upon returning to the classroom schedules, one particular day remains in my thoughts. He was explaining to the class that there are mansions upon mansions of God's blessing that have not even been tapped yet. After the days of blessing the campus had already experienced, I was in awe of this statement.

I never dreamed I would have the privilege of seeing this man again, so I was sad when I told him goodbye at the end of year. About ten years later Alfred and Elizabeth Cawston were invited to our home to stay with our family for several days. Our children were very young and the house was small. I was very anxious about this visit but I was also excited, as this Professor was so dear to my heart. I did not know Elizabeth but it didn't take any time, until all of us grew to love this couple deeply.

Our children loved them like grandparents, as they would take such a personal interest in Craig and Shana. I was pregnant with our third child Rachel. It had been a difficult pregnancy and I had required a good deal of bed rest. Before the first evening had come to an end, it seemed as if this couple had become family members.

They spent a great deal of time overseas, but while in the states even with a hectic schedule, they would squeeze in several days with our family. I would be so excited before they would arrive. The time would fly by so fast, and then they would be gone, and I would go through feelings almost like a withdrawal, as I would miss them so terribly.

They both were such incredible people. The missionary work they had done was astounding, but when they came to our home, they just melted into the scene, taking the children on their laps and loving each of us.

Our family had an appointment one evening when they were arriving. I had put a key under the mat for them, and when walking into the house, Alf had gotten into the refrigerator and was eating some old hotdogs. I was worried for him as I didn't know how long they had been there, and I was afraid it would make him sick. But it was so much like him to remind me he had lived in India for thirty years, and his immune system was far advanced.

One day when he came into the kitchen, I was down on my knees scrubbing the floor. I was a busy mother of three small children with many other responsibilities, and on that afternoon I was weary. I looked up, "Alf I don't feel like I am doing anything that is important for God." His wisdom was so practical and yet so profound. "Patty whatever you do, do it as unto the Lord." Suddenly housework and the daily tasks of keeping up with a young family took on a whole new prospective for me. I have often thought about what he said to me that afternoon and it has helped to put life into a healthy balance.

Elizabeth liked to cook, but because they traveled so much, she wasn't able to. When she came to our home, she knew we welcomed her cooking. Curry was her specialty. She knew we were not fond of curry, but we would put up a great protest. Finally we would coax her to cook up some of her favorite curry dishes. We would go to the super market and find the ingredients she needed. I took delight in watching her in the kitchen, knowing she was having a wonderful day of cooking. The only problem was that she would watch each of us at meal time, wondering why we didn't want several helpings.

Alfred and my husband would take off on their antics, and they would have me and the children laughing into the night. And then when Elizabeth would get tickled about something, it was as if she would explode with uncontrolled laughter. So many wonderful and cherished memories our family has of them. They are both in Heaven now, and missed greatly by their family and countless friends.

Alfred loved his family. He would speak so fondly of his grown children and grandchildren. I asked him once, "Don't you miss your children when you are so far away overseas for so long." He didn't have to pause with his reply, "No because I know they are all happy serving God, and it is only a plane trip away. But when we are together, we have a wonderful time." I have thought of that conversation many times when I see families that live in the same town, and yet times together are miserable.

He would get up before dawn and fix a cozy of tea for Elizabeth. If there were dishes left in the sink, they would be cleaned up. My father was so dear to me, but Alf came close behind.

He had a way of infusing into my inner spirit a love for God. I would listen for him in the kitchen in the morning and quietly slip out of bed. The house would be quiet as family members had gone to work or were still sleeping. He would sit in the big recliner in the family room and I would sit at his feet as he would minister to me one on one. The words he would speak would be so full of wisdom and Godliness.

The last time we had one of these quiet times together we only had a few moments. He looked down at me with those deep set blue eyes. "Patty, when you seek God, pray for his holiness." That is just what I had been asking God for. It was if Alf could look deep into my soul.

As God looks upon the affairs of man, ever standing ready to infuse into the very fiber of humanity those principles of righteousness, how much better this world would be if we followed his example. From the account in Genesis of Satan and one-third of the angels being cast out of heaven, there has been a struggle for mankind from the beginning of time. There is only one God. Satan had the highest station, and yet he wanted to be as God. It is uncomfortable to acknowledge that there is evil in this world, but that does not change the fact. There are those who have given themselves over to evil. We are living in a time when evil is called good, and good is called evil. So many negative voices roar so loudly that one can forget the quiet everyday people who go about life doing good, loving family, and asking God for the ability to walk in his righteousness.

  I have grown into loving the righteousness of God. I long ago learned I fall far short in this walk of holiness. But God looks on the heart, and he sees that desire I have, so life has been a wonderful adventure, as day by day I learn new depths of faithfulness of this Shepherd of Heaven.

  This afternoon, after a good deal of time looking over scriptures and making notes, I needed to finish this chapter. It was a struggle to put my hands on the keyboard. How could I possibly convey those deep thoughts of thankfulness I feel? I went to pick up the mail. This Lord, who has been so faithful, has a way of encouraging his servants to complete those tasks he has called them to.

  A number of years ago, I found a book describing the last five years of Corrie Ten Boom's life. I loaned it to a friend, and for some reason could never find it again. I have often wished I could find a copy. As I began to write this particular chapter on righteousness, I would think about this faithful servant, who has been in Heaven for some time. I have gotten very proficient at finding resource books, but I had the title wrong on this particular book. One morning, as I woke up, I was thinking again about how I could find this particular reference. I went right in to my computer, hit the search button, and scrolled down through the list of books about Corrie. There it was! The book is entitled, "The Five Silent Years of Corrie Ten Boom." I ordered the book and was so happy when it came in the mail. I couldn't take time away from writing that day, but as the evening came, I read way into the night.

  A few days ago, I found myself thinking about the impact God had on this faithful servant who had suffered so much in the German

Concentration camps. Realizing my book shelves had lost "The Hiding Place," I again ordered a replacement.

A few days later the second book arrived. As I quickly opened the envelope, I was anxiously saying, "Oh, I hope its Corrie's book!" As I pulled the book out of the wrapper, there before me was the face of a gentle little woman, who had shown our generations the meaning of forgiveness that only could have come from the mighty hand of God who sees all the affairs of man.

As I thumbed through the pages, I immediately knew I would have to lay this aside for the time being, as the impact of what she lived through was already bringing tears, and I needed to be finishing this chapter.

Many years ago, before our children were born, we lived in a small community in northeastern Colorado. Our small white framed church was out on the prairie in a hamlet called Stoneham. There was an elderly gentleman who was a wheat farmer by the name of Charlie Pierce. He and his wife lived very frugally in a small humble home. He was a very quiet man, in his eighties, who would never have bragged about himself. He had a heart for mission's work. I found out that this gentle old man would be visited by missionaries from all over the world. He was so generous, but it was never spoken of. On a Sunday morning, I always made sure, that I would have the privilege of shaking the hand of this hard working rancher of the plains. His hands were strong and his handshake let you know you were special. His face had a radiance like he had been touched from Heaven and his smile was full of kindness, and I would say his life was full of righteousness.

The Good Shepherd knows that we are like sheep that have gone astray, so that is why He is so faithful to come alongside each of us in our journey. The longer we walk with this Lord who loves us so dearly, we take on his nature, and there is a glow that comes into our life as can be seen by Corrie Ten Boom, and this gentle wheat farmer Charlie Pierce.

4-H Sheep Tragedy

The old lambing shed full of dust and shadow, would seem to give escape from the August blast of heat, but not on this late afternoon. The metal roof, turned to a burnt umber shade from years of Wyoming's brutal January cold and wind, was on this late afternoon, a sun baked oven for me as I worked steadily combing and carding the Columbia Ewe I would take to the county fair.

Summers on the McClaflin farm were filled with long hours of work and 4-H activities. My elder brother Mike, thirteen months older to be exact had a stack of purple ribbons on his bedroom wall from several years of having the great thrill of winning Grand Champion on his prize Hampshire pigs. It wasn't my intent to compete with my brother, but the lonely red ribbon from last year's Columbia ewe just didn't have the same place of royalty in my thirteen year old way of thinking.

The suffocating heat pressed down upon me on that afternoon but the words from my father kept me pressing on, steadily combing, carding, and combing again. Several weeks prior, my father came in for dinner with that look on his face that clued me into to something exciting that was about to happen. "Well Pudden, I was out in the pasture and I saw your Columbia Ewe and checked her out. I think you have a Grand Champion there." That set the wheels rolling. This was my year. I had worked so hard on my 4-H sheep and now my time had come. There would be a purple ribbon on my bedroom wall, just on the east side where the afternoon's sun rays would show her off in all her splendor.

Living on a homestead near the east gate of Yellowstone Park was a draw for friends and relatives from afar. We were blessed with many guests in our home, probably because both Mom and Dad were such gracious hosts, in spite of the heavy work load they carried. Fair time was the busiest week of summer for our family, as we all participated in the 4-H judging activities. My father's Uncle Elmer and his wife, Aunt Lizzie had come the day before. I had spent some time with them last night after supper and then back out to the barn I went and worked late into the night. Mike would come out and check on me and help me some, but most of the time I quietly worked away on my Grand Champion, always with my Dad's words propelling me on.

My Columbia ewe patiently stood on the fitting stand, her head in a leather harness, as I worked with diligence hour after hour. The late afternoon sun was accompanied by 100 degree temperatures that left me dry and parched. The family was all in the house drinking iced tea and visiting with my elder relatives. I was tired. I was lonely and missing out on all the fun. My thirst reached an unbearable level of dustbowl proportion.

I quickly ran to the house, leaving my ewe harnessed to the stand. As I entered the kitchen, I could hear Uncle Elmer telling one of his many stories. I filled a large glass with ice cubes, let the cold water run to the top of the brim and then stood for a minute by the living room door. One minute turned into five, and then I knew I must run quickly back to my champion sheep.

It has been over sixty years since that late afternoon in August, but even now as I pen the words, I feel that same quickening of breath with what I found in the sheep shed that day.

The silence; where was that beautiful head of white wool? As I came into the wooden framed doorway, the first impact of tragedy was the harness pulled tight around her neck, taking the breath out of her body. She had fought against the tethered leather just enough to lose her footing and had fallen off the fitting stand.

I turned screaming with a cry of anguish. A cry from the very depths of me running as fast as my body could fly, "Daddy, Daddy!" The screen door flew open as my father ran through it, my brother close on his heels. Of course they both tried to resuscitate the beautiful prize winning sheep, but she was gone. There was no way to console that young girl with sun baked skin for many days to come.

The look on my father's face coming through the screen door has lived on with me and the recollection is burned upon my memory. The look of concern on his face has come to me at times when I have needed that same mercy and loving kindness from a Heavenly Father who is touched with compassion too for persons who cry out for a father when they least deserve it.

Sunday Morning Trip to Church

One of the family stories that surfaces with my three grown children is a Sunday morning many years ago. It was a cold miserable day, with snow on the ground. What I did not realize when the four of us started out for church that morning, driving down Telegraph Avenue, was that in the night, the weather had warmed up, and by early morning the temperature had plummeted, freezing the partially melted snow. I started up a long ramp which went over the top of Interstate 96. Underneath the snow was a thick layer of black ice which covered the bridge. I lost control of the car as it advanced up on other cars in the same condition. Out of my mouth came only one word , "Jesus, Jesus, Jesus." How many times in my lifetime, have I used that one-word prayer with such intensity, countless times I am sure?

There were other cars at the top of the ramp and I hit the back of the car in front of me. We came to a crashing stop, none of us were hurt, but we were all scared. Sometimes I just whisper the name, Jesus, as I go about the day's schedule just because I love him so dearly and it brings me such a sense of tranquility.

I am sure on that brutally cold day out in Shirley Basin, all alone, as my car was about to hit a snowplow, I was sending up another one word prayer. But, as I look back now, I wasn't alone. The Great Shepherd of Heaven was with me, along with a host of angels who had been called alongside. Scripture tells us that even the demons tremble at the name of Jesus.

You believe that there is one God. You do well.
Even the demons believe and tremble! James 2:19 NKJV

NAMESAKE

A dictionary term for namesake would be "a person with the same name as another, or one that is named after another." This is a compliment to that one whose name has been chosen to be carried on in future generations. When the twin granddaughters were born,

Sandy called long distance, wanting the spelling of my middle name. Elizabeth was named after me, but it is Anna who looks like me. One day I had gone out to Craig's home and Sandy and I were looking at a black and white picture of my wedding. We both were commenting on how much Anna looks like me. Anna was standing by with an amazed look on her face. We have laughed a good deal about her expression. She thought we were talking about the way I look now.

It seems that the term "mother-in-law," takes on a hidden agendas, which is not pleasant. I always felt my life had been blessed because of Lenora Booher, my mother-in-law. She not only was a dear and cherished friend, but I knew I could count on her to pray if I asked for her help. Our third child Rachel Lenora has been blessed to carry on her grandmother's name. I am sure Mom would be full of joy if she could sit on a Sunday and hear her granddaughter preach a sermon.

Along with prayers for grandchildren, I pray for my three children and their mates. It seems almost strange to me, as I love Mitch, Paul, and Sandy as my own children.

Shana came and lived with me in Shell for a couple years. She worked in a restaurant in Greybull where she met a young man who was the chef, and his name was Paul. I knew long before I was told that she was falling in love with this young man. The look on her face was a dead giveaway. She worked the afternoon shift, so by the time she cleaned up, and spent five minutes with Paul, Ha! It would be late when she came home.

I had to be at the office early, so to be able to see the sunrise and say morning prayers my alarm would be set for me to rise before dawn. Shana's bedroom was downstairs. When she would come in the front door, no matter how quiet she tried to be, she would wake me up. I would say, "Go down stairs, do not come in here," but she would come in and slip into bed and begin her round of stories from the days adventures. Of course, I would give in to this nonsense, and in no time she would have me succumbing to gales of laughter. The next morning, I would have to drag myself out of bed, but I don't think I would give up any of those late night talks, as they are special memories now.

Paul and Shana were still living in Seattle, when they called to inform me that their third son had been born and his name was Perry Wallace Lewis. He is such a husky good looking young man with a charming personality and a flair for music and painting in watercolor. I know my father's heart would be glad, in knowing he had a grandson named after him.

I think every member of our family is musical. All three children took piano lessons, but it was Shana who was in it for the long haul. She continued with the piano, and then she got a guitar, ukulele, and took saxophone lessons. Paul played a bass guitar in a local band, so music has been a big part of their lives. On Sunday mornings, it warms my heart as I see Shana leading the congregation in worship from her key board.

I decided early on that this book would be dedicated to grandchildren. As I collected all the complete names, I realized there was a correlation of generations with all of them. Because I have such a deep seeded belief in the importance of many generations of the family, I will list each name as follows.

Erik Steven Booher's middle name is taken from his father Craig Steven Booher. John William Booher is named for his grandfather, John Arthur Booher and his mother's father, William Rushing. Anna Marie Booher is named for her grandmother on her mother's side, Rita Marie Rushing. Elizabeth Eyleen Booher is named for her Grandmother, Patricia McClaflin Booher, which is me. Reagan Michael Booher is named after his Great Uncle Mike McClaflin.

Kameron Elbert Musashi Lewis is named for his father, Paul Elbert Lewis and his grandfather, Elbert Lewis. Gabriel Josiah Isao Lewis is named for his father's grandfather Isao Matsuzaka. Perry Wallace Lewis is named after his great grandfather and my father Wallace McClaflin.

Luke Mitchell Ross is named after his father, Mitchell William Ross. Maximus William Ross is named after his father and his grandfather, William Febus.

ENLARGE YOUR TENT

My heart goes out to parents today, as this is not an easy time to raise children. Of course I love my own grandchildren, but I also take delight in all the other children in the church. When I walk up and down the isle of the grocery store, I am drawn to the little faces sitting in the carts. I can't help but smile, and usually the small children smile back.

What is sad for me is when I see the look of fear on some parent's face. In such a time, when children are so violated by predators, is it any wonder that parents and guardians have to be so careful? When I compare how differently my childhood was out in the homestead community where the children were so cared for by not only family, but neighbors as well, I realize how fortunate I am. Throughout this story, I have acknowledged just a few of those persons who have so influenced my own life.

When I think about the mission trip to Africa where the lamby stories were told each day, the faces of children are still before me. In fact I have pictures setting around my desk of that trip as I write day after day. There were so many hundreds of children each evening as our team was preparing to leave for the day. I would walk through the throngs of children touching their heads and blessing them in the name of Jesus. I knew many of these children would soon be orphans and the ache in the hearts of all the team members is still with them.

Two women who have lived out a Godly destiny for this generation are Corrie Ten Boom and Mother Theresa. The reason I have chosen these two particular saints of God, is because neither of these women had the privilege of being married or giving birth to children, and yet they mothered thousands upon thousands of wounded children through the lives they lived. How many dying orphans did Mother Theresa caress in her arms as the angels came to gently take them to the Shepherd of Heaven? We will not know this side of eternity?

I have often read the scriptures in Isaiah 54 about the barren woman who was admonished to break out in singing. These verses speak of children in desperate situations and they want to be acknowledged, loved and cherished.

*Enlarge the place of your tent, stretch your
tent curtains wide,
do not hold back; lengthen your cords,
strengthen your stakes.
For you will spread out to the right and to the left.
Though the mountains be shaken and the hills be removed,*

*yet my unfailing love for you will not be shaken
nor my covenant of peace be removed,
says the Lord, who has compassion on you."
Isaiah 54:2, 3, & 10 NIV*

CHAPTER 7

VALLEY OF THE SHADOW OF DEATH

For the last several years, not only has our nation gone through the pandemic, but all over the globe it has placed a brutal blow onto humanity. In those first months, when families were isolated in their homes I completed the homestead book. There were many days I would work way into the night hours. What a weight off of me when I finally held that much loved book in my hands.

I had moved into my lake cottage at the first part of last year. I tried to be careful and my family had wished Covid would not come to my door but it did. The outcome of those months, so gravely ill, left me with the awareness of so much suffering all around me. When I slowly became stronger and the brain fog eased up I pulled the manuscript for the grief book off the shelf and now it is in print.

Fear has been a component surrounding this time of sickness. There are so many unanswered questions. Unfortunately, it has also caused a polarization sometimes of close friends. In just the last few months, some of my cherished friends have passed away from this dreaded, Covid. In times like this, when one does not know the outcome, if we have had past experiences where faith and courage brought us through, the memories of those times can bring with it a resiliency to survive it all.

I gave up a long time ago trying to answer the question of "Why." Why would a strong strapping young man die within a few days and I survive this dreaded sickness in my later years with lungs that have been damaged from bouts of pneumonia. Why do some saintly people suffer with cancer for an extended period of time before they go to be with this Shepherd of Heaven?

Without a doubt, down through the ages, this 23rd Psalm has brought comfort in times of sorrow. This passage of scripture has been quoted at funerals across the world.

Life is a precious component, but each of us will face death in many forms either with loved family members, friends and with our pets.

I will share my own experience out in the middle of nowhere that would forever change my own life. When a person comes within a breath of eternity and comes up the side of the mountain of survival hopefully life will be changed forever and that is what happened to me. I do not have fear of that moment when I see Jesus face, I just want to complete the destiny of my own life.

Yea, though I walk through the valley of the shadow of death,
I will fear no evil; for you are with me; NKJV

Car wreck in Shirley Basin

I drove away from home that morning with relief as I saw the sun filtering down through the clouds. Hoping the rays of amber, layered with a soft mist of pink cotton candy softness were a promise of a warmer day than it had been in this northern Wyoming country in early February. I was in for a brutal surprise that would forever change my destiny and with this a passion for life that would ever drive me on.

My UW Extension office was housed in the county courthouse in Big Horn County, right at the base of massive and rugged Rocky Mountains. I lived in a small hamlet of Shell and from the picture windows in my living room I could see right into the canyon, a wonderful place to live for someone like me who loved the beauty of nature.

The University was in Laramie, which was approximately a seven hour drive from my home. Traveling was an ongoing part of my job, as I found myself many times all over the state doing programs. Because I was so used to long trips, I had pondered for days why I had such an unsettled feeling. I had called my mother several days before asking her to pray for me as I couldn't shake this uneasiness. I had a habit of rising early to watch the sunrise coming up over the mountains, as I didn't want to miss the splendor of such beauty.

The Sunday morning, I was to leave, I was up at five, long before I would see the first gray glimpse of dawn. As I sat in my chair, with my gaze fixed on the eastern skies, sadness came over me. Although it wasn't an option, I just wished that I could stay home. Finally around seven, I finished loading my bags in the car and returned to lock the front door. This wasn't a usual custom, but on that morning, I opened the door, looked around to my familiar things, and said, "Good-by little home." I started my Toyota Camry and headed down the hill and began my long track to Laramie. On my many journeys, there was a familiar awareness that angels would accompany me. I would pray that the Lord would send angels to travel along with me, and this morning was no different.

    As I drove through Basin, I realized I had to get hold of this melancholy mood, or it was going to be a very long day. I reached into my stash of recordings and pulled out a tape of sermons from my daughter Shana, who lived in Seattle. On a regular basis, she would send me tapes of her Pastor, Reverend Steve Schell of Northwest Foursquare Church. The topic was on praying many kinds of prayers. I popped it into the cassette player. The words he spoke were like healing salve to my emotions as I drove down the highway. By the time the tape had completed, my mood had been elevated into a tranquil stage, and it relieved me as I calculated I had clipped off an hour of my journey as I drove down into Thermopolis. Driving through Wind River canyon regardless of season is a scenic pleasure. It was always a relief to see Shoeshone laying out there in the horizon, as it was a halfway point. For as long as I could remember, this stop off place was like the very end of somewhere.

    I cruised through the small town, and headed to Casper. For the next two hours, I sang old hymns. There have been times in my life that it seemed as if Christ was sitting in the seat right next to me and this one of those days. The melancholy mood had melted into a feeling of strength and peace, as the songs brought so many memories of a lifetime of experience.

    Just a week before, I had received word that I had been awarded a year sabbatical to complete a Qualitative Research project. I was still so excited about the news and it was going to be wonderful to have time to share my gratitude with friends who had been such a support through all the hard work of accomplishing the task of writing.

Much planning had gone into this week, as close friends I had grown up with, who also worked in Extension would be attending the week long training. We had arranged to have adjoining rooms at the motel. Each of us had stashed junk food into coolers. This had been the arrangement on previous trips, which had proved to be disastrous to anyone staying in the rooms adjacent to ours. We were the greatest of friends, and as the week would become tiresome, the evenings would grow in warmth and much laughter, as old stories were rehashed. I had always been blessed with an over active sense of humor, so my retelling would take on new and colorful dimensions. And of course, being the true blue friends that they were, they would laugh at my antics.

By the time I had left Casper, it was the middle of the afternoon. The constant wind that customarily engulfs this area was unusually strong. Since the sun was still shining, I did not realize, as I drove along, that the temperature had plummeted. As I looked back to the Medicine Bow Mountain range to the northeast I saw dark volumes of seething angry clouds coming down upon Shirley Basin. This was an area surrounded by a mountain that created its own climate. I had remembered my mother commenting in the past, "You don't want to get caught in Shirley Basin when a storm comes up."

Now my mother was one of those homestead pioneers, who took on a form of bravery, not common to the modern day woman. Her words had resonated in my storehouse of memory, and for that reason, if I had to drive through Shirley Basin in the winter; I was always relieved to see the sign, Medicine Bow, 22miles.

My Toyota Camry began to pull to the side of the road, as I quickly realized, the wind had risen to gale proportions. I slowed down and gripped the steering wheel, trying to hold the car in my lane of traffic.

Loneliness seemed to engulf my thoughts which became a

companion with those feelings of foreboding that had left home with me. I began to quote the 23rd Psalm over and over. I had just finished the last verse, "And I will live with you forever and forever and forever." Suddenly, I cried, "Dear God, send me more angels." As I came down a hill, my car must have hit a patch of black ice, along with wind gusts which caused the vehicle to begin a spin that went around and around in huge circles into the oncoming lane. Of course there were no cars in sight, but as I spun around the second time, screaming the name of Jesus over and over, terror struck my heart as I saw coming out of snow flurries a huge snow blow coming directly towards me.

    I was amazed, as I realized I was going to see God at that very moment. Thoughts passed so quickly, and there was an awareness of how close I felt of His presence all through that day. It felt like a dark force had pushed me from behind right to the side of the huge plow. Then the darkness came.

    Someone was banging on my window. I was gasping for air, as the blasts of wind were brutal on my face. I looked up to see a look of panic on a face, of a man I did not know. The winter elements of wind and cold had caused deep wind-burned wrinkles, but he had a look of kindness. I would later feel badly for the driver of the snow plow as he thought I was dead. My car was on the side of the road, with a lone hubcap from the front wheel lying in the middle of the pavement. The snow plow was parked across the highway, the side of the bed smashed and the snow blade bent up into the air. I felt disoriented and all I could think was for him to call my brother Wayne, who lived on a farm near Powell.

    The highway patrolmen quickly arrived. He brought me a small quilt to wrap around my legs. It would take an hour for the ambulance to arrive. As I sat there, with most of the windows shattered, I realized the car was crunched in all around me. My seat was broken, glass was everywhere. I looked down and noticed my stomach had begun to swell. I lifted my shirt, and the entire front of me was purple. Panic seized me for a moment as I knew I was hurt.

Would I freeze or bleed to death out here so far away from my family. Instantly as the thought came, I saw my son's face with such a depth of sorrow in his eyes. My father's memory came to me so clear as if he was right there in the car. I took great strength from the last words my father spoke to me, before his death from the ravages of cancer, "I'll never give up hope, I'll never give up hope."

I quickly assessed my situation and came to the conclusion, "I am not dying today, I'm not cold, and I'm not going to cry. I am going to be thankful for that kind man over there sitting in the cab of the snow plow and the poor fellow out there having to wave the traffic around the debris my car left in the road.

I later was told the temperature had plummeted to more than twenty below. I just wanted to go home, but that was not going to happen, as the roads were closed behind me.

When the ambulance arrived, five volunteers had come to help. By this time, the sun had gone down, and the cold and wind currents had dropped again. The front passenger door had been shoved almost to the middle, so I was relieved they got the door open. A man got in and lifted me up out of my seat as the others managed to get me out from the driver's side. When the full impact of the wind blast hit me, I cried out, but then became immediately sick. The gurney felt like stone and it was hard to lie back, and the last thing I wanted was to throw up, knowing I probably had some broken ribs. I kept requesting blankets, as I couldn't ever remember a time in my life I had been so cold. I was grateful for the many people who helped me that night, but I had an ache in my heart as I wanted my family.

How many times throughout my life, have I discovered the caring of God in some of life's small details that can mean a great deal. My director Glenn Whipple came to the emergency room, which meant so much to me. To my amazement, the local pastor of the Assembly of God, who just happened to be my childhood Sunday school teacher, Dave Garrett and his wife Jean, came and stood by my bed until I had stabilized. I noticed that Dave's arm was in a sling. He had just come through a horrific car accident himself. I knew he was in a great deal of pain, but it was such a relief to me that they had come.

I want to include this snippet of a story of the robin red breast, as it was a source of great encouragement to me in those first months after the wreck. I did not know how badly I was hurt and the pain level was something to be grappled with. I also included the story in the grief book for as I look about me in this season in our nation fear is something that is very tangible for many others on their own personal journey.

ROBIN RED BREAST

February is winter in Wyoming and the sportsman thrives on heavy snows. Shepherds with large flocks of sheep manage to get through the lambing season, and the rest of us hope we can set next to a log fire place in the evenings. And then comes March with a possibility that a few warm and blustery days will let us know winter has almost past.

It was a month after the wreck in Shirley Basin. I was so happy to be in my home in Shell. No complaining came from me, as I was grateful to still be here. I knew it was early for spring, but I couldn't help but look out on the trees, hoping to see the first bud of leaves. The surgeon advised waiting to see how my knees would improve before doing surgery. I was surprised that the bruises had not disappeared. My feet were still a dark purple, and I was for the most part house bound. I was filled with high spirits on this morning as I looked into the long mirror, combing my hair. I had managed to take a shower, what a luxury. Such an ordinary daily process, now took all the energy I could muster. I wasn't discouraged, but the thoughts would come as a question. How would I ever be strong enough to go back to work if this simple task left me so exhausted?

Three picture windows filled the northeast wall of the living room with a view of the west range of the Big Horns. At times birds would be blinded by the morning sun rays and would fly into the windows. As I stood there combing my hair my mind was full of questions. What is going on inside of me? Is there something the doctors haven't discovered? Will my life ever come back to normal? As I stood there, I realized I needed to be done, and lay back down. I heard a loud bang. I went to investigate with Timmy, my Yorky type dog at my heels. As I went to the front glass sliding door, I gently pulled it open. I called Timmy back into the living room as he saw it and had quickly gone out on the deck.

There in front of me lay a little Robin Red Breast. Its wing looked broken and I knew the little bird was stunned and in a great deal of pain.

My pain had already reached the breaking off zone, so as I looked at the bird there, his eyes fixed on me I felt a great compassion for him. What could I do? I must put him out of his misery. I had no weapons in the house. I limped back into the living room, went to the kitchen drawer and pulled out a hammer. As I came back on the deck, somehow I managed to get down on my knees.

There was no way I was going to be able to hit that little bird. I gently picked the little bird up and cradled him in my hands and began to pray. "Dear Heavenly Father, you know how much pain I am in, please let me help this little Robin." He lay very still as I whispered to him, his eyes studying me intently. I laid him back down as carefully as I could and went back into the house. A few minutes later I came back out, anxious for the Robin. To my joy and amazement he was perched up on the railing.

As I quietly came out on the deck, my little Robin Red Breast turned his head back and looked at me. He then lifted both wings and up into the blue sky he flew.

Patricia, March 2001

God speaks to each of us in such incredible ways. He will use the smallest things to speak profound truths to our hearts when we need it the most. For the rest of the day, I felt peace and my faith was reassured as I spoke over and over, "Just like my little Robin Red Breast, I will fly again.

The Lord is my light and my salvation—whom shall I fear?

The Lord is the stronghold of my life—of whom shall I be afraid?

When evil men advance against me to devour my flesh,

when my enemies

and my foes attack me, they will stumble and fall.

Though an army besiege me, my heart will not fear; though war break out against me, even then will I be confident. One thing I ask of the Lord, this is what I seek: That I may dwell in the house of the Lord all the days of my life, to gaze upon the beauty of the Lord and to seek him in his temple. For in the day of trouble he will keep me safe in his dwelling; he will hide me in the shelter of his tabernacle and set me high upon a rock. Then my head will be exalted above the enemies who surround me; At his tabernacle will I sacrifice with shouts of joy? I will sing and make music to the Lord. Psalm 27 NIV

That cold February day seems but a memory to me now. There is one thing everyone who comes so close to death can agree on; you are forever changed as you realize you have been given more time on this earth. From my time as a very young child growing up out on the northern plains of Wyoming, I had an awareness of God, as my loving Heavenly Father and Great Shepherd. Is it any wonder that the stories of me as a little shepherd girl would surface and would come to me with such intensity that I would have to pen them to these pages. I knew the voice of the Shepherd, and I could trust him, as he gave me the courage that day out in Shirley Basin.

After the cold winter day out in Shirley Basin, I was warm again, and life went on, but it was never the same. I slowly recovered, worked hard during my sabbatical year, and spent another year with the University of Wyoming. My eldest is a son by the name of Craig. For many years he had wanted me to come back to

Michigan, not just for visits, but to live. Finally one day in the early morning watching the sunrise, I knew I needed to be near those grandchildren, telling them lamby stories, and investing in them on a regular basis. The decision was not easily made, but much soul searching went into this process.

    Teddy and Ronnie Jones came along side me in the moving process, which always seems to be more difficult than we want to acknowledge. We drove across Interstate 80, with an auto transport in tow. I sat in the front with Ronnie with my little Yorky dog Timmy. Teddy sat in the back seat holding onto their sheep dog with a heavy hand. He was a very smart dog, but he made me nervous, as the look in his eyes suggested, he had thoughts of the tasty morsel setting in the front with shaggy ears.

    Craig, Sandy his wife and my daughter Rachel, her husband Mitch and all the grandchildren met us with open arms that cool and crisp day in late October. I was so hoping there would still be some golden, vibrant red leaves holding on for my friends from Wyoming. So it was with great delight, as we came around the south edge of Lake Michigan my Wyoming friends would be greeted with smashing bright crimson leaves. Life is a tradeoff. Wyoming has the rugged mountains that will always be a part of me. And then we have Michigan with its lush foliage with so many types of trees and lakes, I will never acquire all their proper names.

    I have shared several stories of those times relating to death of flocks of sheep and my prize 4-H animal. More than that, those years out in the sheep barns I grew to love those little bum lambs, giving them names and enjoying all their antics. After so many years, it would seem foolish to remember those times I would be so disgusted early in the mornings, as the eager little lambs would pull off the heavy rubber nipples from the glass coke bottles. I would have to go back into the house and make more bottles of milk because those little orphan lambs were very fragile and they would not be able to go without a feeding.

Isn't that just the way it is with us? As parents, we tend to remember the times we lost patience with our children, forgetting those countless times we showered them with our devotion. And then when it comes to our parents, after they have passed away, we so wish we would never have had tantrums or said something disrespectful in anger. And then when it comes our pets, Oh my goodness, why do we put ourselves through the torture of allowing that little bundle of fluff to come into our home, knowing that for the most part their life span is about fifteen years.

I remember one Christmas I was able to be with my Mom, Pam and Wayne my brother. He and his little Pug had found each other. Whenever I would drive over to the homestead, I knew I would take great delight in watching Wayne and that little Pug, Scooby, who knew he was the center of attention.

The years rolled by ever too quickly and the day came when little Scooby's life was coming to an end.

I had moved to Michigan, but had stayed in close contact, knowing this was going to be a heart break for Wayne and Pam.

I had not been good at knowing how to store my pictures on the computer, so I spent days searching through all the files trying to find those Christmas pictures with my family, with Wayne holding Scooby and Timmy sitting on my lap. After much searching I found the photos and mailed them. Later Pam told me, it had been such a comfort to them. I don't think it was just those darling pictures of Scooby when he was just a little puppy in Wayne's strong hands, but that I shared in the sorrow of it all.

Once again the story would come around to my side of the world. Timmy was eighteen years old. He had been with me in all those years of writing. He would lay at my feet as the hours would roll by as I wrote. When I was recovering from the car wreck. Timmy lay right up next to me, knowing I was wounded. On and on the stories can go. The morning Timmy died, it was Pam that called and walked me through the heart breaking time of saying good-bye to the precious little buddy of mine. My daughter Shana came right over and then Paul and the grandsons buried Timmy out under the tree next to the garden.

The beautiful outcome of that sorrow was that I wrote a book on coping with grief. Of course the title of the book would have to be, "Timmy the Timid, Timmy the Tender, Tools for Coping with Greif." It is a tender and loving story of those times of grief. So it was not a surprise that after months of recovering from the Covid, the silent voice of God would give me the courage and pure grit to finish the manuscript and have the grief book published.

What can we do, when all around us there is heartache, chaos and confusion? Well from my corner of the world, I can pen those deep in the soul and spirit words of comfort and tender loving care for those in the times of sorrow.

Shana's husband Paul is like me. The love for his pets is a set up for heart break, but what does one do? Well we just have our pets and love them passionately and somehow survive it all when they leave us.

Patty, Pam and Wayne McClaflin, Timmy and Scooby

Jango, a Minnie Australian Shepard came into the Lewis home some years ago as a small puppy. He was a very smart dog and with Paul's training, he became a wonderful family pet. The three grandsons, who all understand their father's deep love for his pet had a family meeting over the holidays. "Dad it is time." That was just a few weeks ago so I keep reminding Shana, just give it time.

For many years, I have been interested in studying about resiliency in the human soul. What is that inner component that causes one person to survive sometimes under unbelievable hardship, while others quickly hang up the towel of endurance, lie down and die without a fight?

I wouldn't say that God speaks to me in dreams on a regular basis, but there have been times throughout my life, that He has used this mode of communication with me. I remember the intensity of one such dream relating to my father long ago now, as my son Craig was only two. It was in the middle of the night, the house was silent, I sat up in bed, heart pounding, with my bedclothes soaked with sweat, the heartbroken sobs that came woke my husband with a start. For days I relived the vision of looking down at the face of my father in a casket. The next week we went to see my husband's parents. I had always felt my mother-in-law was a special gift, as we were such dear friends. I was relieved to sit with her that afternoon at her kitchen table drinking cups of coffee. She was well aware of the deep devotion I felt for my father, so as I told her about the dream, we cried together. Lenora was her name and she was a woman of prayer. She spoke with the gentle authority of one who had walked a long journey with this Shepherd of Heaven. "Patty something is going to happen to your Father and we need to agree together to pray for him". That visit was in June, and on a regular daily basis Mom and I prayed for my Daddy.

It was late August when the call came. My dad was at state fair in Douglas, Wyoming. He was down by the river watching the judging of sheep, when the heartache came. I don't think he realized what was happening, as he became sick to his stomach, but he walked up to the 4-H office which was a long climb up several steep hills. He never was one to draw a lot of attention to himself, but he did tell the clerk standing there in the 4-H office he needed an ambulance. I will always know in my heart that angels walked up that hill with Wallace McClaflin that day, along with the Shepherd of Heaven holding his hand. His journey on this earth was not over. He had many miles to walk before he was to go home.

He would remain in Douglas for two weeks because his condition was critical. My brother Mike, got an early leave from the military, drove up through Kansas to pick me and Craig up, and we drove to Wyoming. Daddy was very weak, but for a few moments when we were alone that day in the hospital he shared something that is still with me. I looked down at his weather worn sun baked face. In a weary soft voice he spoke to me knowing his condition was very touch and go at that point. "Pat, there is a man in the next room who has had a heart attack too, but he won't make it. He has given up. I know I will make it." And he did!. It was a long haul for him, as well as my mother and brother, who took over the farming for the next year but he gradually came back to a place where he could farm again.

I am an avid reader. My writing has only encouraged my shelves to grow along the walls of my study with resources. The Bible always tops all other books for personal daily meditation, but close behind in my files one can find research on human resiliency and many other topics closely related. One book that has caught my attention is entitled, "Adversity Quotient," written by Paul Stoltz. I have a great deal of respect for the contribution he has made in research on overcoming adversity. I have recommended this work to many colleagues of mine, dealing with the human resiliency factor

Looking back on the days when I began to write the first shepherd book comes to mind. The last leaves had fallen and winter was upon us. The stories of the lambs would come to me, sometimes in the midnight hours with an awareness that I had to write again. It had been a busy summer going to Kenya, East Africa with the missionary team. The lamby stories from the 23rd Psalm being told to the little African children were but a memory now. I had left all the lamby puppets with the pastors knowing the children had come to love those little faces.

At this point in life's journey I have become keenly aware of how the valley experiences spoken of in Psalm 23:4 bring a depth of insight if we are willing to look beyond our own personal loss and reach out to another passer-by. Cancer has become a common word in our vocabulary but until it hits home within our family or with that forever friend we somehow don't grasp the suffocating pain to our chest, as if we have received a swift and deadly blow.

After that summer of 1986 with the passing of my father, I would see women in the grocery store with the kerchief style hats, faces of gray pallor, knowing they were going through the throws of cancer in some form. But Daddy had been in Heaven for a long time now.

In those few chapters I speak of my friend Virla Harrell. My husband's older brother David was married to Gordy Harrell's sister Barbra. We had been friends for many years and had times of sharing about our love of creativity during those Booher reunions up in the Rocky Mountains of Colorado. Our children were all about the same age so they had become friends riding horses together during those reunions.

When I began the Qualitative Research, Virla offered to help with the audio transcripts as she had past experience. We worked a long time together sharing the stories of the homesteaders. Of course when I began the writing of the shepherd book and needed to return to my roots in the lambing sheds, she wanted to come along and share the experience.

When Virla called that fall to tell me she had an advanced cancer it was evident that she was very ill. In the next few months, so many prayers were prayed for the Harrell family. I was not always able to talk to her, but Gordy would help me in knowing the accounts of what she was going through. There are so many things about sickness like cancer or Covid, that one does not even think about until they or a family member walks through it.

Creativity is one of the modes of coping with grief I have used in many forms throughout my life. As winter was coming on, I got into my stash of felt wool I had previously used in classes I taught. Virla is an amazing artist, so with the hats I designed for her, I would sew in silk flowers and beads. I made her a quilt and worried that it would be too heavy for her, but she told me later it was used often as she would get so cold.

Throughout scripture one can find that when a person cries out to God in desperation, he runs quickly, just as a parent would respond immediately to the cry of a child in trouble. The Bible from the time of the ancients is the lifeblood of man's existence; but in the midnight hour, where else can we go but to the Lord.

In my distress I cried to the Lord,
And he heard me. Psalm 120:1 NKJV

When we look about us and see the wonderful creation God has made and how He truly is our Great Shepherd, why would He leave us at such a time when a loved friend is so close to eternity.

For those of us who have come within a breath of meeting death, life is forever changed. Dimensions of time change for us. We realize this life will pass all too quickly so we must be vigilant in those things we have been called to do. Virla did come through that time of sickness. She still paints beautiful paintings with the gift of creativity God has blessed her with.

DEATH OF A FATHER

As I sit before my computer today there is a picture, faded now with age, setting on my desk. As I pick up the small frame, I know the tears will come, as I can only make out a glimpse of the smile I had loved so dearly from a father who tried, in his quiet way that day so long ago, to give me courage I would need so desperately in just a short time.

I long ago came to peace with the great Shepherd of Heaven with the death of my father. Harboring grief each year on the day he died, July 26, 1986 is not what he would have wanted. But now as I sit quietly with gentle classics playing in the background I am reminded of that time. It would be easier to pass lightly over this passage in the McClaflin family, but for you the reader who is facing that time with a parent, or maybe your own homecoming, I will for a brief reprieve go back and relive that sorrow.

Christmas was almost here, and my parents were coming from Wyoming to spend the holidays and attend my graduation celebrations as I was going to walk down an aisle to receive my diploma for a Master's degree. It seemed like a dream, but it was now a reality.

Growing up on that northern Wyoming homestead taught me many life lessons that I still practice today. From an early age it was understood that my father's greatest desire was to see his children have college degrees. On many occasions as I rose at 4:00 A.M. or studied way into the midnight hours, the look of pride that I knew I would see on my father's face as I reached out to clutch that diploma in my hand gave me a relentless drive.

It had been a blessed Christmas time with the folks and now they were setting in the family room as we were about to take them to catch their plane home. My father suddenly had an excruciating pain in his back. He became so uncomfortable that upon arriving home he went for a checkup. When the test results came back, it was discovered that he had lung cancer and it had moved on to his liver. He was given two weeks, and the maximum time for him would be five months.

Just as I had done years before when my father had suffered a severe heart attack, I asked God to give me a gift of faith. So many friends came alongside our family during that time and prayed. I remember times in the night, I would slip into the living room, moonlight creating shadows on the walls, and I would lie across the carpet weeping for a miraculous healing for this Daddy of mine.

One Sunday morning a lady came up to me after service. She apologized as she handed me a note written on yellow tablet paper. "I am sorry this is all the paper I had one day as I was at work. This message came to me as I thought about you praying for your Father." I thanked her and went off to be alone as I read the words. "Your Daddy has something he wants accomplished and he needs someone to agree with him in prayer." I opened my Bible to the passage she had written down. It read;

Now may the God of hope fill you with all joy and peace in believing, that you may abound in hope by the power of the Holy Spirit.
Romans 15:13 NKJV

How I needed to hold on to hope and I wasn't feeling much joy, so these words became imprinted on my soul.

That night the prayers changed. I wasn't sure what that message on that scribbled notepad meant, but I prayed fervent prayers that my father's desire would be granted. All the family came to Wyoming in June, and on the last night a long table was stretched out in the living room so that every member to the smallest child could be seated. Daddy wanted to stand and bless the meal and the family. I still had not come to the realization that our father would be with us for just a brief time. It is so good to know this Great Shepherd of humanity, but in the valley of death, He has to be the most precious to those who love him. I am reminded of the scripture, "Precious in the sight of the Lord is the death of His saints." Psalm 116:15

A few weeks later our family was at church camp near London, Ontario. It was already hot and humid that morning during the song service. The minister led the congregation in the old hymn, "I Surrender All." It is hard to describe to one who is not attuned to hearing God's voice how clearly He does speak to us. As I sang the words of that beloved old hymn on that old campground the reality came to me. That afternoon I went off alone with an old chair and sat looking out on the lake. For hours I stared at the water. A few days later the call came and my husband booked a flight for me to Wyoming for that afternoon. My heart aches for families, as I now understand the devastation that accompanies watching the ravages of cancer in those we love so dearly. Mike and Linda were missionaries in Africa, so it was a concern that they would make it home in time to see Daddy. Later we would reflect of how God had taken care of the smallest details during the time of our father's illness.

One afternoon I slipped into Daddy's bedroom. He lay so still there, hardly able to speak. The few words I spoke were in such desperation. He looked at me with eyes deep set in his gray face. With a croaking voice barely above a whisper his words burned into my soul; "I'll never give up hope; I'll never give up hope!" How could I possibly know that in just a short while my faith would be tested as it went through fiery trials and years later when I sat out in the middle of nowhere in sub-zero weather with my life on a precipice, those words would flood back as if my father were sitting right next to me in that crushed car. At those times in my life there was always that underlying remembrance, "I'll never give up hope," and that would cause me to hold on to the Lords hand with all my might.

The hours before the ambulance came for my Dad are a fog at this time, but I remember that Daddy didn't have on the pajamas I had gotten him for Father's Day. I spent hours looking for his gift, finally decided on a pair, cobalt blue cotton satin with piping around the collar.

Now they were lifting him on to the gurney, his suffering was unbearable and the faded brown pajamas were frayed around the collar. Of course, I mentioned this to no one. Why would I be so frantic about a pair of pajamas when everything was winding down, and no one could stop it?

In the morning hours the death rattle came. I would slip out into the hall with the kindly nurse wearing a soft pink sweater and she would explain to me what was happening. All of our family was there that July morning with Daddy. I stood for hours there next to his bedside, trying to put into my memory every crease and line of his face.

When death came he just dissolved down into the pillow like an ancient grey tent being folded up, then hemorrhaging came and he was with God.

When families enter into a time of grief, it can take many forms as each individual has their own way of processing loss. Hands down, I have never questioned the unconditional love my brothers, Mike and Wayne have for me. This was not going to be a season any of us would walk through quickly. Each of us would have to come to an acceptance of this experience. Mike and Linda and their three children walked through their grief on foreign soil back in Africa.

Pam and Wayne lived on the farm across the road from the homestead, so theirs was a daily reminder as they would watch mother.

Mom would drive up to the farm just under the shadow of Heart Mountain, the place that was so close to our father's heart and that would somehow bring comfort to her shattered soul.

I remember having to say Good-bye to our mother the morning we flew home. As I put my arms around her, I felt how frail she had become. She was a young widow without her husband of forty-five years.

Patricia and her father, Wallace McClaflin in June of 1986

The Second World War had come to a close. While living in southern California my parents had received the news that the McClaflin name had been drawn first to receive a homestead near Powell, Wyoming. They felt this was their special place on earth. They both had worked hard all their lives. I never had heard my father say he wanted a boat. The fall before his sickness he had bought a fishing boat and let Mom pick out a camper. When they had come for Christmas, he had taken us to a boat store so we could see what kind of boat he had purchased.

His eyes would sparkle as he talked about his boat and the fun the family would have all going fishing together. Mom and Dad never got to use the camper.

A few days after the funeral my family flew home to Detroit. That first Sunday morning after the funeral setting through church was an agony. Roy Crossman's face comes to mind He was a father of six but he often would comment that I was one of his daughters. I remember him coming up after service. He enfolded me in a great bear hug and we both cried deep sobs of sorrow.

What can one say to that one who is in the throes of grief? We tend to want to have answers, but this side of eternity we may never know why one is taken.

As my life has unfolded I have commented many times while in a place of confusion, "When I get to Heaven, I am going to ask the Lord why." But alas as the years slip by, I am recognizing that when we are in Heaven standing in the presence of the Great Shepherd, we won't need to have answers.

THE PIONEER WOMAN, MY MOM

Who would have dreamed ever so long ago when a brother and sister, only six and seven made a trek over the great Rocky Mountains, what life lay ahead for them? It was in the midnight hours riding on that Greyhound bus from southern California with their mother Edna Mae McClaflin when they were awakened to see snow for the first time in their young lives. Their father was anxiously awaiting their arrival as he had gone ahead months before to prepare a home in a primitive Japanese barracks from the Second World War for his family to live in on a homestead with virgin soil in northern Wyoming.

The years have rolled on, it seems faster each year. Daddy left us way too soon in July of 1986 at the age of 67. The cancer took him swiftly. His greatest sadness was in not being able to see his grandchildren grow up. And now I so wish each of my own children and grandchildren could have sat with this man with so much horse sense and appreciation for the simple ways of life.

My mother on the other hand missed her 100 year-old birthday by just thirty seven days. She lived her last few years in a nursing home near Shell, Wyoming where I lived for a number of years while working for the University of Wyoming. We had hoped she could have lived out her last years on the homestead but that did not happen.

Looking back on those first years making paths with my stick horse through the large sage brush not yet cleared on the farmland, I dreamed. My young girl's mind was full of imagination and color and dreams of building and designing and creating beautiful things out of the ordinary stuff of life.

My pet kittens, and then in a few years, the bum lambs I cared for created a place of empathy that would unfold much later in the words penned to pages of writing journals.

My love for designing and sewing began very early, as I would quietly find the paste board box of fabric shoved to the back of the closet. I never asked permission but would cut pieces out and design dresses, bonnets and slippers for the kittens. They didn't seem to mind being dressed up and carted around the farm yard in a doll buggy.

When I was nine, Mike and I joined the 4-H youth program. Our parents both became leaders. Our homestead community all became involved, so this made a great impact on the young people that grew up in the Heart Mountain farm lands.

Those first few years, the stick horse had been replaced by a real live horse named Nosy. I was a Wyoming cowgirl with cowboy boots, and when my chores were done, I just wanted to be out on the hillside riding and dreaming.

Homestead women worked hard, but they still took time to teach the children the 4-H activities. My Mom not only taught me how to sew, but through the years, I suppose she must have taught hundreds of children how to sew.

I remember well the green dress. It was the second year of sewing so my skill level, was basic, along with the attitude of "get me outdoors, I don't want to sit here working on this dumb dress. It took a great deal of coaxing one morning, but finally I convinced my mother to allow me to ride my horse to the 4-H meeting about two miles away. I promised her I would rush right home and finish the dress that evening as the county fair was in a few days.

Well I dawdled on the way home riding up one lane and then another until I arrived home late. I hurried and tied the saddle up in the small barn and ran into the house to do my chores. The dishes were done and I needed to get to sewing. "Where was that bag with my dress and sewing notions?" Then I remembered I had tied it to the saddle horn in my rush to get home as I was late. I ran out to the barn that sat right in the middle of the pig barn yard. In my panic upon getting home late, I had not closed the barn door securely.

As I opened the gate, I could feel my heart suddenly skip a beat. There were those pigs standing in their manure and green tufts of fabric poked out around the yard. I suppose the pigs pulled on the bag and thought the green fabric was grass. Now there were only a few days left, so the next morning off to town we went for more fabric. Honesty, I just don't remember much about the rest of that evening.

That is not the end of this story, for in just a few years, as sewing skills improved, I came to love the sewing projects. Even in those first years, I always seemed to have a flair for individual design.

There are not words that would be adequate enough to thank my Mom for sticking with me in the earlier years. In those years we had Sewing Specialists that came from the university to teach workshops on tailoring.

We raised sheep, so I was familiar with wool. By the time I had graduated from high school, I not only had mastered skills in tailoring but had won trips and honors which challenged me to excellence in design and sewing.

I am grateful that I had the privilege of growing up on a Wyoming homestead and for the impact that 4-H had on my life. Those young people grew up with a strong work ethic and a family closeness, along with community involvement.

I got married and had three children which have truly been the joy of my life. When we are young we have dreams of how we think life will be for us, and for me I saw skies of blue and goodness. Sometimes our dreams turn to ashes, no matter how hard we try to bring peace to a troubled situation.

I came back to Wyoming after many years to take a position with the University of Wyoming but my heart seemed to be shattered in a million pieces. One of the first colleagues I met upon returning was my counterpart, Mary Martin in Jackson Hole, Wyoming. My office was in Lincoln County just south of Jackson. Mary encouraged me, or I could better say coerced me into attending "Quilting in the Tetons," in Jackson Hole, Wyoming.

I walked into that first class, not even knowing what a rotary cutter, rulers or cutting mats were. I didn't want to be there, as tears were just under the surface. But looking back on that time, I would say, "It was the first day of the rest of my life in designing." From that first experience, I would attend every year. I never again took a basic quilting class, but my treasured friend Mary introduced me to the most incredible instructors. In the next few years I learned about silk dying, beading, silk ribbon embroidery, French heirloom sewing and on and on the list could go.

The beautiful story in all of this, is that in those years of sorrow and grief, as I worked with my hands in the skills my mother had taught me as a child, and coupled with the vast horizon of creativity with silks and wool and beads my heart began to calm and the peace that only God can bring gave me courage that one day my heart would sing again.

A few years ago my mother was on my mind and heart. I just wanted to go see her and bring her peace as she was entering a new season of her own life in a nursing home. I flew out to Wyoming and those few days with my mother I will treasure for the rest of my life. As I came home those creative thoughts came and I wanted to make her a wool dress. I went to the storage and there it was just waiting all this time; a beautiful piece of Pendleton ivory wool I had won in a contest.

Of course the design is an original. Night after night as I sewed and thought how much I love my Mom, the design took on a life of its own. I took far much longer then I would have imagined, but that is okay, for as I sewed each bead and created each flower, it was if I was saying, "Mom if I searched throughout the whole earth to choose a Mom, it would be you."

Patricia McClaflin Booher, October 26, 2017

I included this snippet of story of my Mom, as it gives some semblance of those early years of sewing and how it has impacted my life. When our father died, he was still so young. The cancer moved so quickly, and there just was not time to process it all but maybe there is never enough time.

It was different for our Mom as she had lived a long life. She had always been so active, so being confined in the nursing home was a huge adjustment for her.

The wool dress was finally finished. Looking back on those months of sewing with the skills of tailoring my own mother had taught me was a blessing. I knew I was getting carried away with designing the silk flowers and beading, but in those many nights sewing way into the night hours, I had time to grieve for my mother who I knew one day would leave our family.

I so wanted to be able to give my mother her dress because I knew she would understand the love that went into making it. Mike got me a plane ticket and I flew out and spent several days with my mother. One afternoon we had a party for Mom and I got to give her the dress. She asked me, "Patty what will you do with the dress when I pass away?" I held back the tears as I told her, "Mom you are going to be buried in your dress."

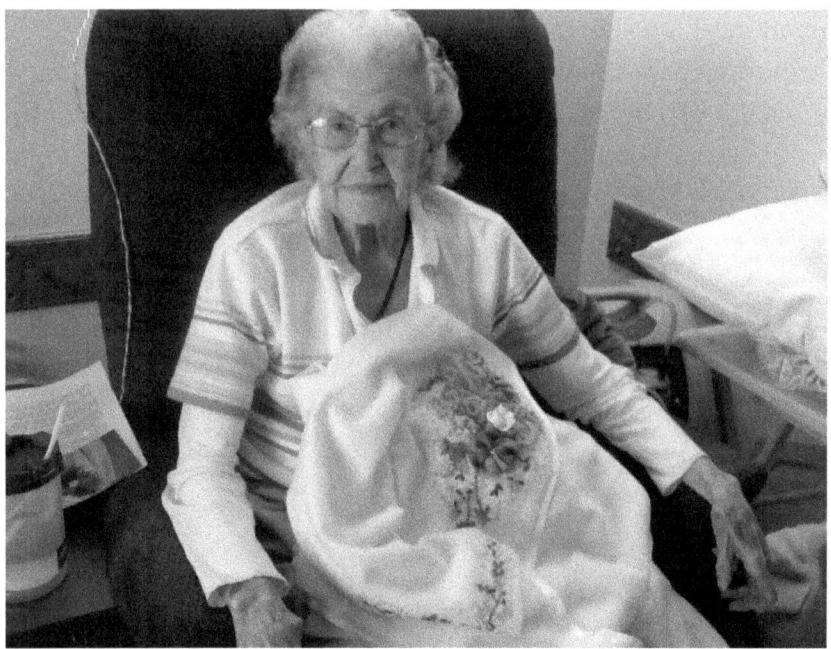

Edna Mae McClaflin, my mom with the wool dress, I so lovingly made her.

The morning I left her, I just seemed to know I would not see her again before eternity. I leaned down, put my arms around her frail little shoulders and she prayed. Oh such a beautiful prayer of hope and courage this little pioneer woman prayed over her daughter.

I have often thought of those words she prayed about the next season of my life. If she were here sitting with me in the spring looking out over the lake and observing the many beautiful terra cotta pots filled with flowers, she would smile

CHAPTER 8
ACCEPTANCE

I have been grateful that I have this picture in my album of memories. It was taken that first time I went with my "Forever Friends," to the condo up in northern Michigan. They have truly been kindred spirits to me for many years. On the left is Pat Vess, Esther Collins, Carol Lemay-Strong and Mary Ellen Fraser.

I have included this portion of my own life story visiting a prison that happened just a short while after my father past away. I was wondering if life would ever come back into balance at the time. My father has been in heaven for many years. I did come to a place of acceptance and now I find that both my mother and father seem to be in those precious thoughts and memories of this shepherd girl.

PRISON VISIT

It was early morning, the family was still sleeping when I left. That Saturday morning in early October had a smell of frost and the air nipped about my face. I would have just as soon gone back and crawled in bed, but then I reflected that I had been awake for hours. It was a sunny day, so I didn't realize the air was full of frost. I slipped quietly back into the house and got a heavy sweater, not wanting to disturb the sleeping house full of family.

I drove to the destination where I would meet Paul Carr, Director of Prison Ministry. We would drive together to the prison. My face was flushed and eyes were swollen. As I looked into the mirror, it seemed as if over-night I had aged many years. Why did I ask to do this? What in the world could I say to those men, in the condition I found myself on this cold brisk morning in the fall of 1986?

Several weeks prior our family had been invited to dinner in the home of one of the team members of the church outreach to the prisons. During this period of time, I was not a very cordial guest, as just getting dressed and arriving was about all I could muster. We sat across from Mary Carducci and her husband Tony listening to them speak of the prison ministry and what it meant to them. I felt ashamed of myself that night, as my own heart ached so badly, I just wanted to go home and pull a cloak of safety around myself. In the next weeks, as I would drive back and forth from teaching, commuting with a van full of children, I would reflect on the words of that very special couple.

It wasn't long before a thought process began to form within me and I knew somehow I needed to make a visit to a prison. The next Sunday morning I found Mary and began to try and explain what I was feeling. "I think the Lord is speaking to me about going to speak to prisoners." She was very kind as she replied that she would put me on the speaking schedule for the women's prison.

Now I felt anxious. "I don't understand this, but I feel I need to go to a men's prison." Mary looked at me, with a question mark written all over her face. "Okay Patty I will speak to Paul Carr and let him put you on the schedule."

Paul didn't waste any time contacting me. Daily schedules that were packed too full didn't give me time to panic on what I had gotten myself into. The day I would go to the prison came all too quickly. I was not ready or prepared to speak to anyone, let alone men dressed in blue ill-fitting uniforms.

I saw Paul's car in the parking lot off of Interstate 96 where we had planned to meet. As I slipped into the passenger's seat of his car I smiled, hoping he didn't see that my eyes were swollen from crying.

When we drove into the parking lot and I looked up at the prison, my heart seemed to take a nose dive. Paul went through the process of registering me. It was time to walk through those heavy iron bars. As I heard the heavy slam of metal against metal, the click of the dead bolt, there was no way to retreat. I would have to face those men.

A torrential rain had passed through in the early morning hours. There had been some flooding in the building we were at, so we had to wait in the guest receiving room for an hour. As I sat waiting, I felt cold and then clammy. As the minutes seemed to move in slow motion I began to feel sick at my stomach. I went into the ladies bathroom and put cold water on my face. I didn't dare let myself cry at this point. "Dear Lord, please help me, the ache I feel this morning is more than I can bear."

I went back out into the waiting room and sat down. In just a few minutes we were ushered in to a room with folding chairs situated in a circle. About twenty men filed into the room. The service began with singing. I listened to hymns sung by men who knew the Shepherd. They sang with beautiful harmony which only tended to evoke deeper waves of melancholy within my spirit.

It was time for me to speak. All I could whisper was "Jesus." He came to me with lightning speed. As I stood there looking into the eyes of those men, I did not see prison uniforms, I did not see men incarcerated, I saw humanity the way God looks upon each of us.

I began to speak in a very soft voice, "I don't know why I am here today, but God has spoken to my heart and wanted me to come, so that is why I came. I don't feel up to speaking this morning, so please forgive me. My Daddy died two months ago and I miss him so much I can hardly breathe. I know he loved me so dearly and that made me feel so special. The Lord has asked me to come and tell you men that you are special to someone, and he wants me to remind you of that. I know it is hard to be enclosed in these prison walls but you must remember that just like my precious Daddy, someone feels about you the same way."

From down in the depths of my spirit came the cry. It shook me as the pressure of trying to hold it down had erupted. The men quietly got out of their seats came around me and began to pray. As the crying subsided, I listened to the most eloquent and beautiful prayers from my brothers in Christ. The prayers came from men, who also had come to the end of themselves. It touched the very core of me.

It was time for us to depart, so I said good-bye in the best way I could. As we drove back to Detroit I apologized to Paul. "Oh Paul I am so sorry, I did so badly, I shouldn't have tried to go with you at this time."

Paul looked at me and the words he spoke gave me a new hope despite the grief I was experiencing. "Don't you realize what has happened this morning? You let those men minister to you, and that has given them a dignity and purpose that is more important than anything that could have been said."

A few weeks later a packet arrived at the church full of messages from the prisoners written to me. Of course they were limited in writing materials, but the letters of encouragement and hope they sent gave me faith that the time spent in this passage of grief would come to a conclusion so I could go on and laugh again with the joy of life. One man sent a small calendar with an x placed for each day until he would be able to be released. I knew it must have been a tremendous sacrifice for him to send it to me. The next time Paul went to the prison, I was anxious to go visit the men. It was so good to see them, and because they had shown me such kindness I was able to greet them with a happy smile and I think a little laugh came up out of me, as I was filled with joy at seeing them again.

Morning Stroll with My Shepherd

There were many mornings in the old vintage home I would strap on my accordion and sing old hymns and worship before a day of writing. For those of us who have a hobby of gardening, the words resound in meaning. I would often quietly sing verses of this song as I made my rounds of early morning watering in the flower beds.

"IN THE GARDEN"

I come to the garden alone,
While the dew is still on the roses,
And the voice I hear,
Falling on my ear,
The Son of God discloses.

Chorus
And He walks with me, and He talks with me,
And He tells me I am His own;
And the joy we share as we tarry there,
None other has ever known.
He speaks and the sound of his voice
Is so sweet the birds hush their singing,
And the melody that He gave to me,
Within my heart is ringing.

I'd stay in the garden with Him
Tho' the night around me be falling,
But He bids me go;
Thro' the voice of woe His voice to me is calling.

Years ago this was a song often sung at funerals. It is common to associate certain songs with life situations. At times I have heard someone say, "I never want to receive fresh flowers, because the smell reminds me of the death of a loved one." I think of the lovely melodies and fragrances that will cease to be a part of an individual's life, and that is very sad. Life seems to take us right where we are at. If we live long enough, we will at some time have a season of grief in some form or another. Grief is usually identified with the death of a loved one. In fact grief can accompany many of life's circumstances, losing a home, divorce, loss of a pet, a failed career.

    I have had a personal relationship with this Great Shepherd of Heaven, Jesus Christ, from the time I was a small child. That has not insulated me from times of sorrowful grief and loneliness. As I look back over my personal journey, I would not ask for those seasons of grief to be taken away.

    As I was looking through the computer files yesterday, I came across a poem I had forgotten that I had written. I am grateful at this point of my life that I had the presence of mind to date all of my writing, as it has been a context later for me to reflect on how my faith was playing out at specific times in my own journey. I found it interesting that the "High Road" poem was written just a few weeks after the wreck in Shirley Basin when I was still homebound. As I examine the words of this poem, I would think that it had been written while setting on a rock at the cattle bridge next to Shell Creek flowing down the mountain side. But in fact, I wasn't able to drive yet, and found myself in solitude for many days in succession. Although I was in a great deal of pain, not certain of what the future held for me, those months at home were some of my most precious times with God. In that season of recovery from the wreck it was if I was the one climbing up that steep mountain path in Shell canyon. The tenacious perseverance and patience I needed at that time had already been infused into the fiber of my human character from past seasons of grief that had passed into an acceptance of life as it truly does seem to take us right where we are at.

THE HIGH ROAD

There is a path along life's journey so few choose to traverse.
A high road sometimes a great distance
From the well-traveled highways of this life.
A road map of this lane many times hard to read.
While walking this path,
One need take heed as the far distant lane is not visible
to the human eye.
It is the path of faith,
A difficult way of self-sacrifice,
An ever increasing personal endurance
That reaches far beyond what can be attained
Within the human frame.
A letting go of those beggarly elements
That engulfs the carefree passerby.
This journey will at times go through craggy cliffs,
high mountain passes;
But when the faithful ascend into the heavenly trails
It is possible to look down on the valley of human trials overcome.
The air so free from the pollution from this life gives
Renewed life to the climber
Who has surrendered himself to difficulties
to attain the highest prize.
All man's senses take on a new keenness,
Bringing with it a clear eye and ear to see and hear God in His glory.

Patricia, March 2001

For the most part parents love their children. We hear the horrific stories of child abuse, but most of us would jump over the moon to protect our kids. I try to attend all the school programs for my grandchildren, but that is not always possible. I look around at other grandparents when it's time for their family member to do whatever. We are easy to spot in the crowd, as we swell up with pride. I think we would all agree, we love those little ones more than life. One thing is for sure, we want to go first, hands down. The sorrow that is felt by parents, when losing a child is hard to comprehend, but hopefully they at some point can go on with life and find a solace.

From an early age, when children can grasp the meaning of death they know that at some time in the future they will be facing the loss of parents. We know this, and yet when it is our mother or father, it is different. How many times have I comforted someone else at the loss of a parent? But when it was my own father, suddenly it took a whole new meaning and depth of understanding.

I have completed writing the portion of this book on going through the valley of the shadow of death. I added two of Elisabeth Kubler-Ross's books to my resource files during these days of writing. Her compassionate handling of the topic of death in "Death, The Final Stage of Growth," gives meaning to the seasons that persons walk through in the death of a family member or special friend. I was hoping I could move right on to the next verse, but here I sit late in the afternoon with classical music playing, knowing I have to share a time in my own personal journey when I just could not seem to get to the next stage of growth and acceptance. What was wrong with me? I had a deep faith in God. My father was in Heaven. I had many responsibilities. People were counting on me. So for a short reprieve, I will go back to a time in my own journey, and roll back the layers of protection, allowing you the reader a glimpse of a time I had drawn the tent of sorrow around myself.

The month before Daddy died, we had brought the family home. The time on the homestead passed too quickly. We were all loaded up in the van but I couldn't leave yet. I got out of the van and went back into the house. Daddy was standing there in the kitchen. He put his arms around me, and I can remember Wayne and Pam put their arms around me too. I should have known that day that the Lord was going to take him home.

If one were to examine me in relation to the five steps of grief, outlined in the work of Kubler-Ross, I would have fit into the stage of denial at that point in June of 1986. In relation to the Shepherd of

Heaven, knowing what would follow the death of Daddy, the Lord was giving me a time of reprieve.

The afternoon after the passing of Wallace McClaflin, the house seemed quiet, although all of the family was present except Daddy. I slipped away unnoticed to the bedroom that had been mine as a child. I stretched out over the bed, unable to cry. It was hard to breathe. I don't know how long I laid there? I didn't hear the door open. Wayne and Pam slipped into the room. He didn't say anything just stretched out next to me and put his arm around me and Pam stood next to him. My brother Wayne was a man of wisdom, when it came to dealing with his sister. They knew I was going to walk through a dark valley with shadows for a period of time. I call him my little big brother, but I am fourteen years older than Wayne. He is well over six feet, long and lanky, dark hair with a touch of gray on the sides, with a smile that always warms my heart. I think he looks like one of those handsome cowboys in the movies. I missed out on having a sister, but I always felt like my two brothers Mike and Wayne made up for it in double portion, along with their wives, Pam and Linda. I think Wayne and I have many similarities. I can just see the look in his eyes and I know he can read me.

Mike and Linda along with their three children had to come to an acceptance of our father's death back in Africa, a long way from the old homestead. After everyone had gone home, Mom, Wayne and Pam had to learn a new pattern of life as they were the ones that remained in Wyoming. The funeral passed by, we said good-byes to loved ones and friends and flew home to Michigan. School started in the fall. I was back to teaching, keeping up with a busy family and going through the mechanics of breathing.

The gift of faith I was blessed with during that season of my father's time with chemotherapy will always be cherished. I have thanked the Lord so many times that He was so gracious to me. A comment was made to me after Daddy passed away, "You're just embarrassed because he wasn't healed after you had prayed so many months." I just let that pass over me, as I would have prayed a thousand times over; I just couldn't seem to get a grip on the ache inside. Another person, uncomfortable at my grief, said after three months, "Are you still grieving, don't you have any faith?"

The human mind wants answers. If we are not careful we give answers to questions of this life that might not ever be answered. It is not comfortable to watch someone else walk through the grief process. At these times we need God's gift of compassion, patience and empathy. If we try to pull another through a knot hole, jumping through the five steps of grief, that person just might miss a time of solitude when the Father in Heaven wants to share golden nuggets of truth only received in a time of grief.

As the weeks passed by I would get up before the sun, walk around the block, around and around I would go. I couldn't get that last morning in the hospital out of my mind, the suffering that preceded the death rattle, and then the hemorrhaging of dark blood coming out of Daddy's mouth. Mike had seen it coming as he said, "Oh no here we go." Nights were filled with tormenting dreams. Life goes on, so the only thing I could do was go to a quiet place in my soul. One morning as I walked around the block with ice and snow on the sidewalk, I prayed and cried, asking my Heavenly Father to help me cope with the grief. His silent voice came to me that morning. "You cannot think any more about the morning he died; I'll put the memory in a safe room and shut the door." As I stood there on that bitter winter morning, an inner strength came to my being. I walked back to the house, fixed breakfast for the family and drove the children to school. I have had to relive that morning in the hospital as I have penned the words to this page, but this is a safe time for my spirit, and I long ago came to an acceptance.

A year after Daddy's funeral, Bob and Diana Allessi, formerly from our church in Detroit, invited our family to Florida. We were given the keys to a lovely condo right on the water's edge. I have always loved swimming in the ocean. I would go out in the morning and swim way out into the water. I swam away from the family as the tears would come and I didn't want them to see me. One evening we were invited to dinner with very dear friends who also were from our congregation in Detroit. They had moved to Florida so it was a special treat to see them. Fred and Georgia King and her mother, Sister Burkholder, who had been my husband's secretary made the evening special for us. I thought I had managed to be my old self, just like old times with these wonderful friends who always had been so good to our family.

The next morning, we left early and headed back home. We had only driven for about two hours. I was grateful my husband was driving as we drove through a narrow pass. There was a river on the driver's side and a large rock embankment on the passenger side. As I looked in the side mirror I saw sparks flying up from the pavement. Suddenly the van began to swerve violently towards the boulders on my side. As John clutched the stirring wheel, he was able to bring the van to a stop. When we got out of the van, we were shocked to see that both tires on the passenger side had fallen off. We were later to discover that the lug nuts had not been tightened when four new tires had been put on the van, just before we had left on the trip.

Bob and Diana Allessi drove out to meet us. The girls went with their father and Bob into a town nearby to get the tires repaired. When I look back on that morning, I know God's hand of safety was on our family, as the van could have rolled so easily into the boulders. I am also aware that my loving Shepherd had heard my heart's cry to him that week as I swam out into the ocean. God had given Diana just the words I needed to hear. "Patty we have all noticed, you are not okay. Your heart is so sad; you are still in deep grief over the loss of your father." Her words were not condemning, but filled with compassion and understanding. The hot tears that ran down my face brought a relief from the weight of trying to lift myself out of the sadness. It was hard to speak, as the cocoon of grief had wrapped itself so tightly around my soul that I had become silent. But I did begin to talk with Diana, telling her how much I missed my Dad.

The next week the girls were off to youth camp, Craig was away on a job, my husband was at the office, and I was home alone. It was almost to the day, a year since Daddy's death. This grief had to pass on, as it was affecting my life too greatly. I went into the sunroom, closed all the windows and began to pray. I hope all my neighbors were not home on that day. There have been times throughout my life, that I would say I have travailed in prayer for another, but on this day God heard my need.

I could no longer be in the stage of denial because death had come. If it took bargaining, then I would have been willing to do anything. As I prayed, I was shocked as I began to tell God, "I am so angry." I don't ever remember acknowledging that in my life before this time. At first it scared me, as I heard the words pouring out of the depths of my spirit. For an hour the sobs came in such violent force and then I was absolutely quiet. I sat there for a long time, grateful for no phone calls, just quiet. After a time the room was filled with the presence of God. It was as if the sunroom became a hallowed sanctuary. I began to tell the Lord how much I loved him and then; "Dear Lord what has happened to me? I feel like there is a huge hole in my heart." The Holy Spirit began to speak to that inner part of me reserved only for Him. "The pain you have felt in grieving for your father has been crushing to you. During the process of grief I have enlarged your heart to love more deeply, to have the compassion that only comes out of suffering."

Later I would find those scriptures that would confirm what had happened to me on that day in July. The KJV has taken on a special meaning for me in Psalm 119:32: *"I will run the course of Your commandments, For You shall enlarge my heart."*
I sat there on the couch for a long time, knowing that my Heavenly Shepherd had walked through this time of grief with me. I came to accept my father's death that day, and rejoiced that he was in Heaven with God. As I stood up I was free. The NIV translation expresses well what I felt. *"I run in the path of your commands, for you have set my heart free."* Psalm 119:3.

The weeks quickly passed and school began again. Some of my happiest moments have been when I was in a class with young people. A weight had been lifted off me. I could see the faces and hearts of the students more clearly. But I was different. It seemed as if I had a keener sense of life, not wanting to miss that one sitting in my class, sad and alone.

SHELL CANYON

Years later when I would drive up through Shell canyon, I would pull the car off the road, look across the deep ravine, and follow with my eyes that mountain path made by the cattle so many years ago. Linda and KL Reed had lived down the hill and around the corner from me those years in Shell. Linda was a true blue friend, who I often read my freshly penned poems to. We enjoyed inspecting each other's gardens, sharing the latest novel we had read, cried together when pets died, and just enjoyed life. I have asked KL about that mountain trail at times, wondering if he had made the trip up the mountain side. "Were you scared KL?" "Well no, but then I didn't want to go up the trail very often and I am accustomed to that type of terrain." KL is one of those cowboys you read about in the old westerns, as he is a horseman in his own right. I enjoyed the little community of Shell. As I would take walks in the evenings up towards the canyon, I would take note of the cowboys as they would drive by in pick-ups still working late into the evening. There was always a dog or two standing on a bale of hay in the back.

It was a wonder they never flew out, as they would wind up and down those mountain roads, but they seemed to have glue in their feet as they would bark at a passersby.

Shell canyon is a deep ravine along the mountainside. As travelers make their way up the switchbacks; the top of the mountain comes into view. I call the massive rock formation that covers the top of the mountain Table rock. It has been named by others, "The Tomb," to each his own. When I was a young child making trips up the North Fork with my family, we would identify all the rock formations that had been given names. It took a lot of imagination at times to formulate how someone had named a certain set of boulders. But this is how it is done out west. We have names for boulders, hillsides, and mountain passes.

There was a hill I used to climb just down the road from the Reed ranch. I don't know that it had a name, but it looked very much like a large muffin made from batter that had been stirred too much. The climb to

There have been times in my own journey in life, the mountain trail of circumstances have been difficult. At times a passerby has asked me, "How do you make it?" The best way I have been able to express my approach to life is, "I get up in the morning, say my prayers, ask the Great Shepherd for my marching orders, put on my boots and start marching."

As I look back over my life's' journey I have had, I would not want to take away any season. Both in Wyoming and Michigan, when the middle of February arrives, the southern beaches are looking really good but the four seasons are so special. I wouldn't want to miss out on seeing those first yellow and purple crocus popping up in the back yard, swimming in Lake Michigan with the grandchildren, watching the explosion of fall colors and seeing the excitement and hearing the laughter of children at Christmas as snow lays its lovely coating of white on the evergreen trees of Michigan.

Throughout my journey there have been those friends I call my "Forever Friends." This is one of my favorite poems as it so depicts how felt soon after the car wreck in Shirley Basin.

FOREVER FRIEND

Seasons come and go,

Spring, summer, fall, and winter,

A time for crying and time for laughing,

A time to be silent, a time to speak.

In all of these seasons there is glue that runs down

into the crevices of the soul,

And upon the open wounded places of the heart.

This adhesive is what brings courage

in the most trying of times,

Brings a smile upon a face masked in tears,

Hope is renewed because of this glue,

An ointment so valuable no price tag

can be placed on it's worth.

What is the glue you ask?

Let me tell you in a hushed tone of reverence.

This is my forever friend.

That one who believes in me when I am discouraged,

Who sees beyond today and helps me remember my dreams.

Forgives me when I don't deserve it,

Will cheer me on when I pursue the destiny and visions

for my life,

Will grow old with me,

And we will remember the seasons fondly,

The tears, the laughter, the disappointments,

and the triumphs,

The spring, the summer, the fall, and winter,

My forever friend and that is you.

Patricia McClaflin Booher, May 1, 2001

"WINTER ROSE BUD"

The last rose of summer

I had the privilege of being one of the family members who spoke at my mother's funeral. I did manage to get through what I had written down. In those days of planning with the family, I received a call from Mary Ellen's daughter Mary, telling me that my precious friend had passed away. I was so honored that the family asked me to be one of the speakers at her funeral. In having two of those in my life, that meant so much to me, die so close together in time made me appreciate the experience with the last rose of summer in the fall.

    I have enclosed those words I spoke on that day for my friend from so many wonderful years

TRIBUTE TO MARY ELLEN FRASER

    Our young family came to Detroit in 1976 to become the Pastors of the church that would later be called Fairlane Assembly. The church building was on East Warren in Dearborn. Coming from a homestead out in Wyoming and then living in Kansas, it seemed this was the biggest and scariest city in the entire world. Oh how we so quickly came to love this congregation of hard working city dwellers.

    Although our youngest child Rachel was only three at the time, our children remember in vivid memory those nights after church in the parking lot as the adults would visit out in the hot August evenings for it seemed to them eternity.

    Jim and Mary Ellen and all of their family immediately became dear friends. It seems so long ago now, but as I pause to think back, Mary Ellen was always there by my side in all the adventures of pastoring.

    When I returned to Michigan in 2003, life was much different for me. I still had the residual effects of a heart so broken. This did not deter in any way the friendship of this precious friend Mary Ellen. If anything it only caused her to come even closer as that "Forever Friend." It seemed to both of us that all those years apart had been as of yesterday.

    I was still recovering from a near fatal car accident a year before returning to Michigan. Although I had loved our congregation, life was now very different, so there was a foreboding of how it would be for me, but after the accident my family knew it was time for their mother to come back home to them.

    Early on Mary Ellen began to tell me of this cottage in the woods up north and four friends who would love me just as she did. Well, it took months of coaxing me, as I wanted to stay way in the back side of the stages of life. The day finally came for our group to drive up north. As was my custom, I had hot cinnamon rolls coming out of the oven for them to have before we started out on our trip.

    Pat Vess drove her SUV and the rest of us enjoyed the scenery. There was Mary Ellen Fraser, Esther Collins, Carol Lemay-

Strong, Pat Vess and myself on that trip and there would be many trips to follow.

In my mind's eye I was thinking of a little log cabin in the woods. As we drove up the winding hill and looked at this beautiful two story condo, we all were overwhelmed. Mary Ellen's daughter Ellen had made this possible as it was a vacation home she and her husband had purchased.

The next few days the bonds of friendship evolved into becoming prayer partners in the five of us that became so strong it would last all these years.

Upon returning to Michigan, I had purchased a beautiful old vintage home out in Jackson. The sun room was filled with windows and mellow golden oak floors. Mary Ellen would come to see me upon occasion.

Being the farm girl I will always be, I love to bake. I took great delight in making all those things I knew Mary Ellen enjoyed. Her favorite was the lemon meringue pie. The first time I brought the piece of pie still warm from the oven, she exclaimed, which so was like how I describe Mary Ellen, "Oh I feel so guilty, this is wonderful, but it was Jim's favorite."

On those mornings sitting out there in the sun room eating hot muffins and drinking tea, I would read to Mary Ellen the chapters of the book I was writing at the time on the 23 Psalm. One of those rare and priceless qualities Mary Ellen always possessed is that she was an empathic listener. That is a person who has the ability to listen from the heart. This would give me courage to just keep on writing. Even now, I would dare say that will be one of those qualities I will always cherish and miss so terribly from this friend so dear to my heart.

We often shared the stories of our children and grandchildren. We shared in the success of all of them and prayed often together for our families. Although some of Mary Ellen's children have not seen me for a long time, because of those many times with their mother loving them so tenderly I feel a deep kindred spirit to each of them.

I had a little Yorky type dog named Timmy that was my shadow. Mary Ellen informed me she really did not like dogs at all.

Well she forgot to tell Timmy. As I would be in the kitchen fixing whatever for our morning time in the sunroom, Timmy would somehow make his way up on her lap and before long, she really did come to love that dog, as I would see him snuggled down under her quilt and then come and lick her face and she would be smiling.

When my book, "Reflections of a Wyoming Shepherd on the 23rd Psalm" was completed I took a book tour out in Wyoming for six weeks in the late spring of 2009. I had left early in May so my garden out in the back had not been taken care before I left on my trip. I was very concerned that I would not be able to find any flowers left in the shops when I returned in June.

It was after midnight when my Yorky dog and I drove into my backyard in late June after a very long book tour. I came up on the deck, opened the door, turned on the light and looked out on my back yard. I walked down into the grass noticing all the flower beds were freshly manicured and the lawn was mowed. I did not realize at the time that Mary Ellen and Carol Lemay-Strong had come out and spent all day pulling weeds and getting ready for planting flowers. And yes, I did find a wonderful flower nursery late that June morning. What amazing friends I have had, I am blessed so far beyond measure.

Carol and I decided we would take our friend Mary Ellen to Lake Michigan. When we arrived at the parking lot we loaded up all the chairs, umbrellas and food containers and we started down the long walk. Getting through the sand was very difficult for Mary Ellen. We spent a wonderful day, the three of us, but getting back up the steep hill of sand was going to be very difficult. We did not notice the beautiful lady with dark hair sitting there on the wooden bench. She came down and asked if she could help us. She loaded all the chairs and other heavy items we had and walked briskly down the side walk, we managed to get Mary Ellen up out of the sand. We looked around and did not see the lady. Carol and I looked at each other with amazement. We both asked each other at the same time, "Did we just see an angel." When we got to our car there were all our beach items neatly stacked in a row.

For about six years I lived in an apartment. The administration had allowed me to develop a garden in the forest that I could see from my second story deck. For Mother's Day every year, my son Craig buys me a rose plant. That year the roses were a deep scarlet hue with layers upon layers of petals. It was a late very warm fall this season. I made my early morning trek out to the garden to check the plants, knowing there would be a heavy snow late in the night. I saw the stem reaching way up taller than me with one rose bud at the very top. I so hoped it would be the last rose of summer. I took a picture of the rosebud and when I went to the computer, I saw that the light was over exposed. As I sat there looking at the small rose bud with light shining down on it, it seems I could hear that silent voice of God speaking to me.

"Your mother and Mary Ellen are now closer to Heaven then to earth. Very soon they will be with Jesus."

A few days later I went back out to the garden, and there was the rosebud, now frozen, but with awe I looked at the leaves still holding on in a deep beauty of veins in emerald green. Once again that silent voice of the Shepherd of Heaven comforted my heart that was already taking on the grief of a mother and friend so loved.

"The blooms of the lives of your mother and Mary Ellen will bloom now in Heaven and oh what beauty it will bring."

My mother, Edna Mae McClaflin died on November 27th, 2019 and Mary Ellen Fraser, my cherished friend died on December 9, 2019.

A Message for Mary Ellen's Children

Jim, Scott, Don, Greg, Ellen, Mary, wives, husbands, and grandchildren.

Sometimes life does not end as a Hallmark card. Sometimes there is sufferings and questions we have of "Why did this happen to Mom?" Mary Ellen would say:

"Oh my children and grandchildren give yourselves time to grieve, but remember the beauty of the leaves of winter as beauty of life as you have each been loved unconditionally and that will last for an eternity. I am now so young and much nearer then you can imagine. I have seen the face of Jesus and at last after so many years, I am with the love of my life, your father Jim"

When I look back over the years after I returned to live in Michigan, my four friends I have labeled "Forever Friends," were always my great support whether writing, recovering from surgery or just enjoying life together. Before this last Christmas, I had been doing a good deal of writing and designing the journals. We did not get to visit that often, but on those mornings we did connect on the phone, Pat Vess and I would have the most beautiful conversations. I could tell by her voice that she was very tired, so I didn't visit long with her. One morning I checked into my Facebook and saw a picture of Pat blowing out candles on her birthday cake. I thought, "Oh Goodness, her birthday has slipped up on me." As I began to read the message that Monday morning, I just could hardly believe it. My dear precious friend Pat Vess had passed away. I called Mary Ellen's daughter, Mary. She quickly shifted her day around and came and got me so I could attend the funeral that evening. As I am finishing this chapter on "Acceptance," of this edition of the Shepherd book, I would so love to call my friend Pat and share with her, but in my heart I know she is well now, sickness is behind her. Pat Vess ended well on her journey in this life that brought beauty and love to countless friends and family.

Finally, brethren, whatsoever things are true, whatsoever things are noble, whatsoever things are just, whatsoever things are pure, whatsoever things are lovely, whatsoever

things are of good report, if there be any virtue, and if there be anything praiseworthy, meditate on these things.
Philippines 4:8 NKJV

CHAPTER 9

I WILL FEAR NO EVIL

Fear is a part of the human frame that has to be grappled with. How many writers, painters, or great leaders have given up because fear came into central focus, and all dreams were lost and hope was gone?

When I wrote the first edition of the shepherd book, fear was a component I wrestled with. I would get up early and pray out in my sunroom. That silent voice I knew so well would speak those thoughts of what I was to write that day. Thank goodness I have come a long way from those first writings, as my mind would be filled with such intimidation and yes I will call it fear. When I could finally just put my hands on the keyboard it seemed I would write like the wind.

I have come to the conclusion that fear is something we will face at times throughout our journey here on earth. Past experiences of coping and overcoming those foreboding thoughts can build faith within this human frame and a resilience and pure grit to just get up and be about our destiny.

The first writing for the shepherd book that came out of my spirit was penned to the page and with the thoughts that came, a confidence that I would once again have the privilege of expressing my devotion to this Shepherd Heaven through words that displaced the fear.

I have included this portion of writing, "What If," that had been formerly written. As I read through the words, it very likely was written on one of those days I was needing to accomplish something and I had to overcome the fear that is the unwelcome visitor in the human frame.

WHAT IF

My hands are on the keyboard. I have turned my chair, so I can't see the piles on my desk. How many times in the past have I been in this same frame of mind. Knowing something had to be written down before it was lost to never return. The same fear, how well I know its face, the droning on of, "What If." What if my mind turns to glue?

What if someone reads this? What if this pounding in my chest, isn't real? But then I know what it is, as I have traveled this passage way too many times on my journey. Just to grasp and hold on tenaciously to that inner strength that has gotten me through many a storm. To acknowledge my faith in a Faithful God who has always been there. Knowing he speaks in whispers so quiet at times, it takes the discipline that comes only through personal integrity of that one who develops character through the crucibles of the hard seasons of life to be able to hear.

Do I have anything worthwhile to say? Is there a painting in my mind, if not completed that will never find its way upon a museum wall to be admired long after I have breathed my last breath. Is there a child somewhere longing for my smile? Is there an elderly lady, hands aching with arthritis that should long ago be retired checking out my groceries at the end of a long day? Just a look into her weary face, "Thank you and you have a nice day." The faint smile passes quickly, but she has felt the caring of someone who acknowledged her as a person of worth.

"What If? What If? What If?" I have finally made it to the keyboard today. I knew that this was the morning to hide myself away in my cave of writing.

I have a habit of rising early every morning to say quiet prayers and read the Bible. After my devotional time this morning, I began going through the same agony of blocking out every distraction. I picked up a well-worn book loaned to me by a friend several weeks ago. Many times in the last few days I have read words from this author, realizing I needed a copy of my own to mark up, as every page is full of rich thoughts of courage and living one's destiny.

The book had taken on special meaning, as the gentleman who loaned the book had willingly shared with me a portion of his life's journey. I was so moved by his incredible strength of character. He also has books to write. What if he doesn't write down his story? What if he never realizes the impact he will have on humanity?

What If? What If? My attention turns to you. What is that passion within you? What is that thing only you can do? What if you let life, with all its detours steer you away from that inner voice ever calling you to a higher place. If the dream and vision is there then you have been entrusted to bring it to pass. Have a good journey, fellow traveler. I will be standing in the wings cheering you along to your greatest gift that is waiting to unfold.

Patricia Booher, June 23, 2008

I recall a childhood memory of a night when a pack of dogs got into the flock of sheep in the west pasture. I could hear the barking from my bedroom window and I went into my parent's room and woke my dad. He immediately got up and drove over to the pasture. The next morning, my father described what had happened. "They didn't kill the sheep, they just ran alongside of them, and ripped open their intestines." What a terrible thing for a shepherd to witness, in a flock that had been so cared for.

Dogs are in many ways like humans. They can be nice and friendly, but when they get into a pack, with the intent of overpowering a flock of defenseless sheep, all reason is gone. How many times throughout history have we witnessed the brutality of man against man when mob mentality has taken over?

Through the many years that Teddy and Ronnie have raised sheep, they have also had to deal with predators. Ronnie commented on the portion of scripture, "Fear no evil."

"Sheep have no protection of their own except to run away from their enemies. That is why they need a shepherd to protect them and to keep the enemy away from them. As predators attack the flock and scare them they begin to run. If one sheep gets scared, then the whole bunch will follow and they may run over a cliff or into a hole and pile up. A shepherd needs to be watchful to keep his sheep from running away and keep the predators and other things that may frighten the sheep away from them."

In previous verses, the importance of walking in God's righteousness shows his caring for his sheep. Man by nature is willful. Walking with this Shepherd of Heaven in obedience is a day by day practice. We at times forget that he wishes to bless mankind with goodness and peace.

God is the same yesterday, today, and forever. He is like the solid granite boulder I sat on near Shell creek several years ago. He is not moved by circumstances. Scripture declares that the very hairs of our head are numbered. The Bible is God's inspired word breathed to us by the Holy Spirit. The importance of putting the knowledge of this book into one's mind and heart on a daily basis has been proven to me throughout my journey with this Shepherd.

Guard my life and rescue me; let me not be put to shame, for I take refuge in you. May integrity and uprightness protect me, because my hope is in you. Psalm 25:20 -21 NIV

One of my personal experiences that proved the power in the words of the Bible was when I lived through the wreck in Shirley Basin. The night before I left on that particular trip I was restless and had a sense of fear. I was standing in the kitchen with my small suitcase, counting out the vitamins I would need for the week. I had turned on the T.V. and the Hour of Power with Robert Shuler came on. I was busy getting my travel items ready, when the words of the sermon, permeated my thoughts. I stopped and listened to the verse that was being quoted;

For I know the plans I have for you," declares the Lord, "Plans to prosper you and not to harm you, plans to give you hope and a future. Jeremiah 29:11 NIV

Something stirred inside my heart. I went over and stood by the T.V. and began to cry. I knew that God was speaking to me through those words. As I continued packing my bags I found myself settling down, and began to quote a well-worn verse that had encouraged me at other times.

"Do not fear, for I am with you; do not be dismayed,
for I am your God.
I will strengthen you and help you; I will uphold you with my
righteous right hand." Isaiah 41:10 NIV

I don't understand why some things happen. I learned a long time ago I don't have all the answers. But I do know that God is always with us, and in the hardest of times that is when he becomes the most dear.

From the time I was a small child I have loved the 23rd Psalm. I am in awe that I have the privilege to write a down in the heart story surrounding this ever loved scripture. It is not surprising that the day I would be driving into a brutal snow storm, the words would be on my lips,

"And I will dwell in the house of the Lord forever,
and forever, and forever!"

When you pass through the waters, I will be with you; and when you pass through the rivers, they will not sweep over you. When you walk through the fire, you will not be burned;
the flames will not set you ablaze.
Isaiah 43:2 – 2 NIV

When I regained consciousness after colliding with the huge snow plow I was bewildered and so very cold. "What is going to happen to me, am I going to freeze to death? Then the inspired words from God came to me again, "You have a future and a hope." As the faces of my family came into my mind, I began to regroup, knowing my destiny had not been completed, and I would survive this day and have a good journey.

I was relieved when the ambulance finally came, as it was getting dark and the temperature was dropping very quickly. I was taken to the hospital in Laramie. Everyone was so kind to me. Steve Aagard, Assistant Director of Extension, and Mark Ferrell, Extension Specialist, who had hunted with my dad for a number of years, went and took all my personal belongings from the car. I never saw my car, but Steve would later tell me, "I don't know how you could have lived through the wreck." I was greatly relieved when Steve told me he was going to drive me up to Powell to my mom's homestead. I don't think either one of us will ever forget that day of driving, as we both knew that many angels had been with me on that cold night in Shirley Basin.

My brother Wayne, Pam, and Mom were waiting for us when we pulled in that night. I had a brace on my knee and I wasn't looking all that good. Wayne was so kind as he said, "Patty why don't you just go ahead and cry. I think it will help you." There were times I cried from the pain, but I never cried about the wreck, as I felt such awe, that I still had breath in me.

A few days after the wreck, I could hardly breathe as the pain in my upper back was so intense. Pam has an insight that has at times helped me a great deal. She took me over to Cody to see the surgeon, and sure enough ribs were broken.

The brace on my knee was so big I couldn't get my clothes on, so we went to Wal-Mart to look for some sweat pants in a huge size. She got me into a wheel chair and if the long wide aisles were clear she would race me from one end to the other. It felt so good to be able to laugh with my sister, as I think it was a good therapy in getting my mind off of suffering.

The Lord is my light and my salvation, whom shall I fear?
The Lord is the stronghold of my life of whom shall I be afraid?
When evil men advance against me to devour
my flesh, when my enemies
and my foes attack me, they will stumble and fall.
Though an army besiege me, my heart will not fear; though war break
out against me, even then will I be confident.
One thing I ask of the Lord, this is what I seek;
That I may dwell in the house of the Lord all the days of my life, to
gaze upon the beauty of the Lord and to seek him in his temple. For
in the day of trouble he will keep me safe in his dwelling; he will hide
me in the shelter of his tabernacle and set me high upon a rock. Then
my head will be exalted above the enemies who surround me;

At his tabernacle will I sacrifice with shouts of joy?
I will sing and make music to the Lord. Psalm 27 NIV

Craig had been a football and wrestling coach for a number of years. Since the season went into late fall for football, I tried to dress very warm for the grandchildren's games. But wrestling is another story, as it is a one on one sport. I tried to be brave; knowing this was good for the young people, but I think grandma just turns into putty when it comes to those kids. It was the last tournament of the season and all the schools had come to Napoleon high school. It was a big day for Craig, as he was heading up the event as well as couching his team. I arrived to a packed gymnasium and was so glad I could set with Sandy. There were four wrestling mats, so it was a packed gym full of parents and grandparents all cheering for their children. John, my thirteen year-old grandson had hurt his arm in earlier matches, and now they were going into the final tournament of the season. After his first match, the pain was incredible. He is strong like his father, so he went into the second match and won. By the third match, he was miserable, but won again. If he had decided to sit out the last match, I don't think anyone would have criticized him. But he went on to wrestle his final match of the season. Sandy and I couldn't stand it; we went down by the mat. I am sure with all the shouting no one could hear me and hopefully no one noticed me. I began to pray that John would be courageous and not give up. I am sure his mom and dad were praying too. He fought valiantly and he won. The Napoleon team won the tournament. John's arm recovered and life came back to normal. But that day as I looked around that gym and saw all those family members cheering for their own children, I couldn't help but think that in future days; those young people would have fiber built into them to face the challenges of life.

Those Moments of time With the Children

Moments in time can be etched on one's mind by those pictures taken by the family member who is faithful in preserving the family story. Time has moved quickly when I look back on those many years of working with the children. It was my turn to teach the children at Tuesday School. I taught with Ben Poxson, Children's

Ministry Director. I enjoyed the time with him, as I saw the love he had for the young children. They ranged from ages four to ten. Being a lover of creativity, I always brought some type of hands on project for the children to make that enhanced the Bible Story. Regardless of how the craft turned out, it was important to the young children. A memory verse would be printed on a label and adhered to whatever we made. Ben came directly from work, tired, but he was such a great sport. One night we used Elmer's glue to stick fabric to cardboard. It was to be a small replica of the tent Abraham and Sarah lived in, described in Genesis. By the time we got done, it didn't look much like a tent. The glue wasn't very dry on Perry's tent, so a drop or two remained in the family van.

One year we had a Vacation Bible School program. It was all about pirates. Many people in the congregation helped to decorate for the occasion. It was a huge success, as the children talked about it for some time. They learned many wonderful songs. Ben brought the CD up to the children's church room. Every Tuesday night the children wanted to listen to the CD, sing-along, and do all the actions. I was organizing the tent project, as the children sang along with their pirate CD. I went over and sat down and watched the children. Four of those youngsters just happened to be my grandchildren but all of the children called me Grandma. Mitch and Rachel's four-year-old son Luke was holding a microphone singing, "My God is so big, so strong and so mighty, there's nothing my God cannot do." The other children were on the area rug singing along and flexing their miniature muscles. As I listened to Luke, such a serious face, singing all the words with perfect pitch, I said, "Ben we have got to get a video of these children singing." It was one of those moments in time. Knowing the powerful words concerning God's strength was being placed deep in the hearts and minds of those young children refreshed both Ben and me.

There have been times I have sat with a client, or parent, and at times friends who have lost a child to teen-suicide. What can one say when the parent tries to communicate the depth of sorrow they feel. There will be no more sports tournaments for their child, no grandchildren to look forward to, and no dreams that will become reality for that child. In those times I have spoken very few words, but have become a listener and prayed somehow the parents would be able to take deep breathes at some time in the future.

I feel I have been given a gift as I look over the shelves in my own library of books on resiliency. I have listed some of my favorite resources that I have been able to apply in the work I have done with families. Why someone comes to the place that life becomes so hopeless is an interesting question. When fear has come into my life, accompanied with a sense of hopelessness, I have run quickly to the Shepherd of Heaven. But of course, I knew I had the opportunity to do this. I am sure the passion that burns within me to complete this manuscript is heightened with the desire to share simple stories of life that might just give someone else a sense of hope, when despair has over taken them.

RUSTY RESCUES WAYNE

I've always felt one of the special parts of growing up on a farm was the privilege of having a variety of pets. Mom tended to lean toward the kittens. Daddy had a sheep dog named Rusty. Like the other farmer's dogs in our community, Rusty had a special place in the front seat next to my Dad. In those years aluminum tubes were used for irrigation. I used to help pick up the tubes and carry them to the next field, but Mike was the one who could get the suction of water from the ditch up into the tube and down the irrigation rows. I never did get a good handle on that job.

Rusty was Daddy's shadow. He would run up and down chasing the water as it was turned into the ditch. Watching this dog in his play always brought a great deal of enjoyment to our father. Rusty would be covered with mud when the old pick-up returned to the house. In those days the living room had hardwood floors. It was a big job keeping up the waxed shine with dogs and many other things coming into the house. Over by Daddy's rocking chair was a spot easily detected where Rusty, his faithful sheep dog sat.

He not only was a trusted pet, but Rusty was a working sheep dog. He would be called a herder type dog. He could run out and gather up a flock of sheep in no time. At times I would take him to the field with me as I watched out for the sheep. It was a great help, until my Dad would come out of the house. We could be in the back pasture, but if Rusty saw him, I was sunk, as off he would go running to the house to be with my Dad.

When the irrigation project was designed out on Heart Mountain Homestead community canals were used to transport water for irrigation from Buffalo Bill Dam, west of Cody, Wyoming. There were canals next to each homestead unit, as well as a large fast moving canal called Alkali drain which ran through the back of the McClaflin farm. It was a run off of waste water from the farms along the canals. A good deal of water ran down this canal and there were some deep holes. Parents were always concerned for the safety of their children because of the canals.

One day in early spring when Wayne was barely three, he was playing out in the front yard. Mom kept an eye on him as he played, but then when she looked out he wasn't there. She went out right away, feeling something was wrong. She looked everywhere, calling him. She looked in all the barns, calling and calling, "Wayne." She began praying, feeling frantic, and worrying about the canal out in front of the house. The hired man, Dale Watts came to the house and began to help Mom search. As he went out by the sheep shed, he heard Rusty barking way off in the distance. He went out in the back of shed and could see Rusty way down by Alkali Creek. He began to run as fast as he could as the dog was barking furiously. Rusty was running back and forth, jumping in the air way down by Alkali Creek. When Dale got down to Rusty, the dog was jumping on him barking and barking, and then began to run off down the canal road. Dale ran, now feeling panic. When Dale came to where Rusty was barking, he could hear Wayne crying. He looked down at the canal and saw my little brother down in the cold water trying to pry his little coat loose. He was so scared and cold from the rushing water. As he struggled, he had dug himself deeper and deeper until he was in a very desperate situation.

Dale tore his coat loose from the fence, picked up Wayne, and hugged him tight as he was carried back to the house. And of course good old faithful Rusty was following right beside him watching out for that little boy who is much taller than me today.

ELK HUNTING TRIP

Some of the homesteaders in the Heart Mountain community came from local areas, but most of the families came long distance to claim a unit. That first year away from family was hard on everyone. We all felt homesick, so within our community was created a sense of family. The McClaflin name was the first application that was drawn for the homestead project. I remember often, our mother said, "Wallace and I just felt that God had blessed us, and this was our chance to have a farm." When they came to Powell for the interview process, they were accepted as candidates to choose a farm.

Families in the community opened up their homes for these young veteran families. My parents stayed with a delightful lady named, Mrs. Bosley. They were introduced to her daughter Bessie Hoff, and her husband Felix and daughter Phyllis. That was the beginning of a lifelong friendship. They became our long distance family. They had a ranch up near the foothills of the Beartooth Mountain range. Christmas was spent with the Hoffs in the old log home in the Paint creek valley.

Phyllis was six years older than me and I thought she was the most beautiful and important person in the world. She felt like Mike and I were her little brother and sister. When I was in the fourth grade Melanie Hoff was born and then two years later Colleen Hoff was born, and so they were like my little sisters.

Clearing off sage brush and beginning a farm out on the prairies of northern Wyoming meant long exhausting days. The few times we did get to go to Paint Creek in the summer were special times for our family. Felix would saddle up the horses and Phyllis,

Mike and I would ride off for great imaginary adventures up in the rocky ledges.

Late in the fall, Dad and Mom would go hunting with Felix up on Bald Ridge. There was a deep ravine called the Natural Corral. There were several deer paths down into this deep ravine, but if it began to snow one did not want to be caught in this area as the massive rocky cliffs made an enclosure that was impossible to get out of.

When interviewing Mom, this is one of the stories I wanted her to share. "The most memorable hunting trip for Wallace and I was with Felix Hoff. We went up to Pat O'Hara and set up camp with tents, and brought horses with us. That first night of camping, the men had put the tents right on the edge of an old abandoned saw mill. The wind came up in the night and the sawdust blew right into our faces. The next morning we got up early and rode the horses up on the top of Pat O'Hara. I remember how cold it was and I wasn't about to complain, as I was so glad to get to go on this hunt with the men. My face got wind burned that first morning out.

The temperature began to drop during the day and Felix became concerned about his house on Paint Creek as he was afraid the pipes would freeze. It was the last of October, and it seems that back in those years it got cold a lot faster in the fall. We rode over Bald Ridge and down through the Natural Corral to get to his ranch. We spent the night and the next morning we were going to ride back up to the camp.

During the night it began to snow. The men asked me, "Do you want to stay here at the ranch?" I wasn't about to stay there and miss out on the hunt. "No, I'm not staying here, I'm going with you."

We began the trip back up to our campsite. We took the horses up through the Natural Corral. There were only two ways to get in. There was a trail below the corral, and up on top a horse could come down a narrow passage way. It was a rock formation that encircled about a hundred acres deep within the ravine. It was a good place to hunt for deer and elk. Fortunately for Wallace and I, Felix had hunted this territory for years, and knew all the trails

We decided on our way up to the camp we would hunt down in the Natural Corral. Wallace and I took the horses, and Felix went on ahead to spook the elk down into the ravine. Felix left us about 11:00 A.M., and after a long while Wallace began to get nervous, as the snow was coming down so heavy. A heavy fog was rolling into the canyon, and we had no way of knowing how to get out. We kept trying different paths, but would come right up against the rock ledges. The snow was up to the bellies of the horses, so Wallace thought he would leave me with the horses, and try to get out on foot. But he came back in just a few minutes. "Edna it is getting so cold and I don't know if I could ever find you, we had better stay together."

About 4:00 P.M. we heard a gunshot. It sounded like it was right above us. We answered with a shot back. Felix shot back and then he started calling us. He was up on top of the ledge, so he guided us up out of the corral. When we finally joined Felix, he told us the only way we would get off the mountain was to follow the fence line.

Felix was a good guide. He found the fence and we followed it. We came up on a big herd of elk, but we knew our situation was a serious one. There was no way we were going to try and shoot one. At about 9:00 P.M. we got into camp. Felix said, "If we don't try and get out we will be stuck up here for the winter because all the roads will be closed." We didn't have a four-wheel drive, just the old Dodge pickup loaded with rocks for weight. We were all just starved so we quickly ate something and loaded everything in the back of the pickup. Felix instructed us to turn the horses loose, as he said they could find their way back to the ranch. Sure enough a few days later, they returned home.

The camp was about a mile from the road. Felix got on one side and I got on the other, and Wallace drove. We shoveled a path for the wheels because the snow was so deep. It was the old dirt road, not the one that we drive today going to Sunlight. We needed to go to the top of Dead Indian which was about five miles away.

Felix and I would sit on the back end and Wallace would drive a little ways and the chains would break. There was some bailing wire in the back we used to tie the chains together. They kept breaking and we would just be inching along. We got into Paint Creek ranch about 2:00 in the morning. I can still remember how relieved we felt when we drove down the hill and saw the old ranch house. Wallace and I never forgot that trip. I think we both gained an awareness of the mountain storms and how they needed to be respected. Without a good guide, we would have been lost and probably would have frozen to death up there in the canyon. We had many good hunts with Felix in the years to come, but never had another experience that was as frightening as our first hunt in the Natural Corral."

Felix and my parents spoke of that special Elk hunt many times through the years. As I think about the circumstances of that trip down through the Natural Corral in such a heavy snowstorm, I can't help but feel there was a heavenly presence guiding Felix and my parents to safety.

Chapter 10

YOUR ROD AND STAFF, THEY COMFORT ME

Ronnie brought out his staff and showed it to me and then began to explain how it aids him with his flocks of sheep.

"When we think about the rod and staff, the rod is used to protect the sheep from damage from predators or other bad things that might happen to the sheep. The staff, of course, is used to help protect the sheep and also to catch them to be able to doctor whatever illness they may have whether it would be lameness or some kind of cuts or damage around the head and to also possibly protect them from flies and other pesky things that might bother them.

The staff is usually a stick with a curve on one end that can also be used to catch the sheep and bring them back into the flock when they might attempt to stray. They can be caught fairly easily, usually around the neck. It doesn't hurt the sheep but they can be turned and brought back into the flock."

After Ronnie and I were finished taping his interview, he took me out to the corral with his sheep dog and his staff. Later when I reviewed the video taken of his demonstration of how the staff is used, it made me aware of its importance in protecting the sheep. He would go near the flock with his staff and pull out one sheep. This is used when a sheep needs to be taken care. If flies are troubling the sheep, ointment can be applied to the head. The staff does not hurt the sheep, but it is a good way to work with sheep individually.

While living in Shell I would see the sheep herders out on the mountain side leaning on their staff, watching over their flocks of sheep. The staff is usually made out of wood. Sometimes they are carved into ornate designs. In Bible times, the staff was a very important tool herdsmen used with flocks of sheep.

The rod is carried by the herdsman to protect the flock from predators. I once had the privilege, while in Kenya, East Africa, of

Ron Jones holding a shepherd's staff

watching some Maasia herdsmen demonstrating their ability to throw the rod, which can bring a deadly blow to a predator. In modern times, the rod would be referred to as the gun carried by ranchers when working out on the range with cattle and sheep.

While living in Shell, it was not unusual to see coyotes coming in close to sheep in the pastures, and they certainly were close by in the high mountain ranges. If one coyote is visible, there are usually several others close by. They will circle around the defenseless sheep that has wandered off, and without the close watch of a shepherd a good number of sheep can be killed.

In all the years I traveled through the mountain ranges of Wyoming, I have only seen one wolf, and it was in Yellowstone Park. I would not want to be out walking and come upon a wolf, as they are very dangerous. One morning I found footprints of a mountain lion outside the house.

I had been coming home every evening after work and taking long walks up into the hills. A rancher told me the lion wouldn't bother me, but after that I quit walking. When I walked down to the post office to get my mail, I would take a long tree branch, which could be considered a rod, and stay in the middle of the road because as I walked down the hill, rattle snakes would sometimes be crossing the pavement. I enjoyed living near the mountains in Shell, but I always knew I needed to be wise and pay attention to my surroundings.

It is noted in this verse concerning the rod and staff, not only does the Lord want to protect us, but bring us comfort as well. The staff can be a demonstration of the inner man where the word of God is our light and guide in the path to righteousness. The rod can serve as that protection from outside forces that draw us away from the voice of the Holy Spirit that watches over us continually. The Lord warned of those who would come to deceive his lambs. As one is faithful in studying the word of God and praying to have a pure heart, faith in knowing truth is so timely in this time when it appears too often the evil is called good and good is called evil. The teachings of Christ in the three years he walked on this earth ministering are still with us, written under the inspired hand of the prophets. He knew what was ahead for his twelve disciples, and he gave a warning.

Watch out for false prophets. They come to you in sheep's clothing, but inwardly they are ferocious wolves. Matthew 7:15 NIV

A great deal has been invested in you and me, and God is not willing that any man is destroyed. One of the most useful tools given to mankind is prayer. The Lord can touch hearts that are hardened, and cause them to be as soft clay in the potter's hand.

Humble yourselves, therefore, under God's mighty hand, that he may lift you up in due time. Cast all your anxiety on him because he cares for you. Peter 5: 6 & 7 NIV

It is the desire of the Heavenly Shepherd to bring peace and comfort, and the way this is possible is to have a tender heart in the presence of God.

Create in me a pure heart, O God, and renew a steadfast spirit within me. Do not cast me from your presence or take your Holy Spirit from me. Restore to me the joy of your salvation and grant me a willing spirit, to sustain me. Psalm 51: 10 – 12 NIV

We hear the comment, "There is nothing new under the sun," and for the most part that is true. Satan has not changed his tactics from the dawning of time. Therefore we do not have to be afraid, but just as I was careful of predators while living in Shell, we need to honor this God who sent his son, that we might have life and have it **more abundantly.**

Be self-controlled and alert. Your enemy the devil prowls around like a roaring lion looking for someone to devour. Resist him, standing firm in the faith, because you know that your brothers throughout the world are undergoing the same kind of sufferings.

Peter 5:8 NIV

Rachel's husband, Mitch Ross

     If I had a verse in the Psalms that would describe my daughter Rachel's husband Mitch, it would be "Your Rod and Staff they comfort me." Not only has Mitch been a servant, loving father and protector of his wife and sons, but he has been that special friend in my life. He has always been that support and encouragement to me throughout all these years and for that my heart is blessed.

CHAPTER 11
YOU PREPARE A TABLE FOR ME IN THE PRESENCE OF MY ENEMIES

Many years ago when our young family had moved into a new area, we experienced an evening that was very frightening. We were hungry for grilled hamburgers, so we bought a small hibachi and briquettes. There was a lovely park with a creek meandering through it, just a few miles from our home. We loaded up the children, and had the picnic supplies in the trunk. We were all hungry and it seemed like it took forever for the coals to get red hot so we could grill the hamburgers.

We played with the children out in the wide expanse of well cared for lawns. At first, we did not pay attention to the cars and motorcycles pulling up and men dressed in black leather coming around us. In just a few minutes there was a mass of men with dark and sullen expressions glaring at us. We were at the wrong place at the wrong time. We took the hibachi with briquettes, just turning white, and dumped them into the creek, picked up our supplies and children, and walked as inconspicuously as possible through the throng of angry men. We were still frightened when we got home, and the idea of grilling hamburgers had left all of us. We never went back to that area, and later wondered if we had unwittingly chosen an area where drugs were being sold.

I can think of another time when I did not feel safe. This is the only time I can remember in the many trips I took across Wyoming, that I had this kind of experience. I had been working late and headed home over the mountains after dark. I pulled up to a restaurant where I had stopped many other times. I walked into the large dining room and saw a group of men sitting over to the side. They turned and stared at me with expressions that made me feel cold. I sat down, but before the waitress came with water and a menu, that voice I know so well spoke inside of me. "You need to leave this place immediately!" The command was so clear that I got up, did not look over at the group sitting there watching me, went to my car, locked the doors, and headed out as quickly as possible. I didn't make any more stops until I pulled into my garage. I settled for a peanut butter sandwich and hot tea that night, just glad to be home and thankful for the Shepherd always watching out for his sheep.

On a lighter side, one of those gifts passed on to me from my parents is the sheer pleasure of cooking and entertaining in my home. Baking is at the top of the lists of my favorites. I don't think I have ever bought a pie crust. I am always on the lookout for deep dish pie pans. I always have to make cherry pie for my grown children, but after that pie is made, I can branch out to coconut cream, apple crisp and many times experimenting with new recipes. I make mincemeat pie once a year, with all kinds of chiding from my family. Whenever I have dinner guests, I wait to put the croissant rolls in the oven after the guests have arrived. The smell of yeast rolls baking in the oven brings pleasure that is hard to explain. There is something special about setting around the dining room table with friends and family. I enjoy eating in restaurants, but dinners have a special intimate place of friendship in the home.

All of our family likes to cook. I have a nice sized kitchen, but when all of the family comes they like to take part in cooking and it becomes crowded. We take great delight in some of Paul's specialties he has brought from Wyoming. He and Craig would have to be considered chefs in their own right. Rachel makes unusual and fun things, I have never heard of. When friends ask me about my cooking, I just say, "I am the farm girl cook.

I found it interesting in those many interviews with the homesteaders, then almost in their 90s, how often they mentioned that looking back on those first years of farming, the family would sit around the kitchen table for meals. After TV came along years later, often the family would load up their plates and watch a TV program. The comment would often be made that they wished that had not happened.

In this present scene we find ourselves in, with masks, being shut away in lockdowns and then add the component of texting at any cost, the outcome many times is a feeling of isolation and loneliness.

BISCUITS AND CREAM

On the McClaflin homestead there were always some barnyard cats. Every summer I managed to adopt one or two kittens. The only criteria I used for my choice of kittens was that they had to be willing to be dressed up and enjoy riding around in the doll sized baby buggy. Mornings and evenings the cats would stroll out to the small shed where Mike milked the cow. I grew up taking delight in Mike's antics. He had mastered the skill of squirting the milk right into the cat's mouths as they sat there in a row. Well almost mastered I should say. The cats didn't seem to mind, as they would later clean themselves up and lick each other's faces until no one would have known the difference.

Those simple pleasures of growing up on a farm were the sources of many enjoyable moments in the early years of childhood.

Mike would carry the bucket of milk to the well house, where I would pour it into a cream separator. This would separate the cream and milk. Mom made butter and cottage cheese and some of the cream was sold to the local creamery in town. It was important to wash and sanitize the separator as soon as the job was done, as the milk would sour very quickly, and then it was a slimy process which was not pleasant.

Not all of the cream was separated from the milk which was stored in a gallon glass jar in the refrigerator. About an inch of cream could be skimmed off the top when the milk got cold. Cooking for a hungry family and hired men alongside my Mom was hard work. Getting the work done on the northern farms of Wyoming with a short growing season took the help of all the family members. I didn't realize what a privilege was afforded me until later when cooking for large groups of people came naturally to me.

The homemade ice cream, chocolate cakes, and biscuits made with heavy cream were a regular menu in the McClaflin household.

When I could no longer have heavy cream at my disposal, I had to find a whole new assortment of recipes to cook with.

I remember one Booher family reunion that was held in the mountains up near Grand Junction, Colorado. We were driving from Detroit, Michigan, so we stopped in Fleming on the way and stayed with Mom and Dad Booher overnight. Dad took me out to see his new purchase, a beautiful Jersey cow. He sent me off the next morning with a quart of heavy cream. While at the family reunion we stayed in an old trailer with an oven. I was delighted with the gift of cream, as I had not been able to make the childhood recipes for a long time.

I would get up early in order to make biscuits from the cream. One morning I noticed one of the guests wasn't eating biscuits. When I asked him, he said he didn't care for biscuits. The next morning, I said, "Why don't you just take a bite of one of these biscuits? He reluctantly took one of the hot biscuits off the plate. As he took a bite, his face broke out in a smile, "Oh My goodness!" he exclaimed. I didn't have to ask him again for the duration of the reunion, as he would take several on his plate every morning.

Many years have passed since those biscuits made with pure cream right off the farm. It wouldn't do for my figure at this point, as I don't get the physical exercise I did as a young girl. I am grateful for this season of my life, writing down those cherished memories of another time.

Eating is a vital part of survival, but when one has to eat in a place where they do not feel safe, or among persons who are hostile, or even considered an enemy it is not a pleasant experience. If a person finds themselves in constant upheaval while eating, it can affect good health, and also decreases one's appetite.

Ronnie gave a good analogy to his flocks of sheep in relation to this verse, "You prepare a table before me in the presence of my enemies. In Psalm 23, it speaks of the Shepherd preparing a table before me in the presence of my enemies. I can think of an example when lambs are out in the fields. If there is a predator, they will not go near. They are not comfortable, so they don't eat well and they are always watchful and they are not at peace. As long as the predator is close by, whether it is a dog, coyote, fox, wolf or whatever the predator might be, the sheep cannot be comfortable. The sheep doesn't have any protection except getting away from the predator and the danger they are in. As shepherds we have to give them a table of green pastures to eat in that is safe and not infected with predators or other things that distract the sheep like flies and other nuisances for the sheep. When we put them out into a field they need to have the peace and comfort in knowing they are not going to be molested by predators."

"Sheep have many predators. They have internal predators and they have external parasites and predators that chew on them like face flies, which bother them considerably. They walk around with their head down close to the ground trying to keep the flies off of their head. Today we have insecticides that we can use to keep the flies away from the sheep. Before insecticides were available, shepherds used to put oil on the sheep's head to keep the flies away. This would last for two or three weeks and then they would have to retreat the sheep."

YOU ANOINT MY HEAD WITH OIL,
MY CUP RUNS OVER

I am humming to myself, "You Never promised a rose garden." As this song depicts, life is full of surprise and sometimes disappoint. It is easy to fall into the thought process, "If I do things right, am honest, work hard, follow the Ten Commandments," then my life will be without trial. Unfortunately, this is not usually the case. Throughout scripture you and I are admonished to look to God as our source of strength, and to live justly.

As we stroll back through history we can find persons who lived through great difficulty, and yet they remained strong in their faith. Two of my favorite chapters in the Psalms are 37 and 91. When days seem to get hectic, or I find myself fretting, I just sit quietly and by the time I have read the last two verses of chapter 91, I am ready once more to get up and be about the Master's call.

He will call upon me, and I will answer him; I will be with him in trouble, I will deliver him and honor him. With long life will I satisfy him and show him my salvation. Psalm 91: 15-16 NIV

I can think of no moment more blessed then when one feels the touch of anointing from the Heavenly Father. It can come while strolling by a dark and cool mountain stream. It can come in the early morning hours of prayer while the hush of evening dew is still in the air. I have seen this anointing presence touch saints as they stand in the sanctuary lifting holy hands in adoration and worship.

No other human emotion can convey with such depth the feeling of personal worth, tenderness and consuming love that one experiences in those moments of anointing. I have found in my own life experience, that the touch of anointing I felt as a young child has remained with me all of my life.

As a very young girl, I can remember my mother singing in the choir in the Methodist church. I grew up cherishing the old hymns. One particular melody comes to mind as I am writing today. I would be so moved by the words of this song that I would weep setting there next to my father listening to my mother's beautiful lyric soprano voice.

THERE IS A BALM IN GILEAD

There is a balm in Gilead
To make the wounded whole,
There is a balm in Gilead
To save my sin sick soul.

Sometimes I feel discouraged
And I feel I can't go on,
But then the Holy Spirit revives my soul again.
If you cannot preach like Peter,

If you cannot preach like Paul,

Oh, you can tell the Love of Jesus
You can say he died for us all.
There is a balm in Gilead
To make the wounded whole,
There is a balm in Gilead
To save my sin sick soul.

    I woke early this morning, with a song on my mind. I haven't heard it for years and don't even remember the title, but it has to do with the anointing. It is a beautiful song, penned by one who surely has experienced this very special blessing from God.

    In my early morning prayer time, I reached up on the shelf for my volumes of the Psalms by Charles Spurgeon. This collection has been a cherished gift from a friend from many years ago now. All day I have brooded over how I would express this brief passage, "You anoint my head with oil, my cup runs over."

    One of the great joys of a parent is to watch their children grow into fullness and give back to humanity. Rachel falls in line as the youngest, and she has become a Minster. She has an ability to teach the Bible in a way that gives insight and meaning in today's society.

Pastor Rachel Ross

My daughter Rachel has been my pastor all these years, and the value of the impact on my own life cannot be measured in earthly terms. She has walked alongside me in the good times, in times of sickness, and challenged my personal growth of choosing to walk close to God.

I have often wished that my mom and dad could have heard their granddaughter preach the sermons so full of wisdom and Godliness. They would have been so thrilled.

As parents, we tell our children, even after they are grown the impact they have on us as parents, but I don't know that they really grasp at the time the depth of it all. When I came back to live in Michigan, I had the residual effects of the car wreck. I was so happy to be near family. As I look back on the years that have moved ever so quickly, there were many seasons I found myself tucked away writing.

When I wrote the first shepherd book, the only way I can explain the emotions is that I just felt raw at times. As the words I penned to the page were so deep in my soul. One day I was telling my daughter Rachel how emotionally raw, I felt. She said, "Mom I think that is right where you should be." Just hearing those words gave me the courage I needed to just keep writing.

I have always been drawn to the Psalms. Many mornings in the quiet stillness before the rising of the sun, making sure all the windows are closed; I strap on my old accordion and sing praises to God. There is something that brings a portion of the divine down into the rooms of a person's home, which has come to love this Heavenly Shepherd when they worship in song.

Throughout the Bible we see the importance of anointing. The ceremony of anointing was used for kings and priests. Old Testament prophets were touched with a Heavenly anointing. As we read throughout the New Testament, we note the special anointing that followed the Apostles.

I find myself once again tucked away writing a second edition of the shepherd book. I feel such an urgency to have this story finished, as I look around and see the state of affairs in our nation and around the world.

     I will reflect on Stephen and the circumstances that surrounded his becoming a martyr. Acts 7:54-60. There was a young man on the sidelines giving consent to Stephen's death by the name of Saul. As one reads the account of Stephen in his last moments on this earth, he was not concerned with himself but prayed for those who would stone him to death. *"Lord, do not charge them with this sin."* Acts 7:60. If one were to look into the face of Stephen that day, what would they see?

     Although there would be blood gushing down his body, the anointing of Gods glory would have shown on his face as it states he was full of the Holy Spirit and he said, *"Look! I see the heavens opened and the Son of Man standing at the right hand of God,"* and it says, he fell asleep. What a homecoming it must have been on that day Stephen came home to his maker.

     Saul was a religious man, doing what he thought was right. He was persecuting the church. Many saints saw their death because of Saul. What a powerful story of conversion we see in the life of Saul, who was later named Paul in Acts chapter nine. Because of his devotion to God, Paul would later make a pivotal point in propagating Christianity throughout the world.

     I find myself pouring over the epistles written by the Apostle Paul. Through the years, the words penned have empowered my life. I am brought to tears as I realize the last years of his life were in a prison cell. At times he would ask his friends to bring him a coat, as he was cold. As one follows the life of Paul, it is apparent an anointing of God's spirit was like a mantle over him. To see the transformation of thought from chapters 7 and 8 of Romans has been a flagstone in my personal life. The challenge to press on to a higher place in God gives humanity a hope and future. Paul's death came when he was beheaded for his testimony for Jesus Christ. I am sure with Paul's homecoming, standing very near the Shepherd of Heaven, was Stephen with arms open wide ready to receive him.

The Bible in its entirety is my highest treasure. I have carried a reference study Bible in my traveling bag for many years. My first edition marked throughout with scriptures that became a road map in my own life's journey was left in Russia with a new convert. I began again with a NIV translation, marked it up, and left it with my secretary Dori, who had not only been my faithful comrade in the work place at the university office, but a cherished friend for many years. So once again I sit on this early morning in my office with a window that looks out on a frozen lake in January with another reference study Bible. My mind is full and the thoughts come rapidly to me.

On my bedroom wall in front of my bed is a picture I have carried with me for many years. It was given to me by a lady named Carolyn Haley. When she came with the picture, she explained it was something she had treasured, but the Lord told her she would be giving it away. So when our family was moving from a congregation we had cherished for many years, she came with the picture. How could she know at that time, what a comfort this picture would bring to me? This afternoon I took it off the wall and brought it into the office to study one more time. As I study this little shepherd girl, my prayer is that I will have the courage to write about this anointing of oil that begins at the top of the head and flows on down to the feet, forever changing one's destiny and knowledge of God.

Early and late as I look at the picture on the bedroom wall I find myself studying the girl, dressed in blue, watching over the flock of sheep on a hot summer afternoon. It is a simple frock she wears with a well-worn straw hat to protect her from the heat. She is a little shepherd girl who has been instructed by the Shepherd to care for the sheep. How many times has the soft voice of the Shepherd encouraged me to watch for the little lambs in the form of children, touch an elderly person's hand, or hug a crying mother?

I am trying to remember when I first felt this anointing from God's hand on my life. Some of the first recollections would be when I was riding my horse out in the Wyoming prairies, alone with my thoughts, and they were often on God. I would look up into the billowing clouds in the sky and feel his presence in such a way that my soul and spirit would overflow with a sense of love being poured out as an anointing of oil.

Our family attended a small church in my hometown of Powell. The pastor's wife was such a tiny little thing. I think she wore size three shoes. I would always sit with her. There was an old alter that stretched out across the front of the church. After service I would go and spend long periods of time praying. She would kneel down beside me and never leave me. So many times as I prayed next to this saint I would feel the presence of God's anointing. The congregation called them Brother and Sister Thiemann and I knew they both loved me dearly. At times I would feel such joy; I cannot describe it in words. At other times as this anointing would come to me, I would have deep sorrow as I sought God.

Travailing in prayer is rarely mentioned today, but in those years as a young child, I truly believe that is when God was teaching me to seek him in my times of prayer at the alter and out riding my horse in a solitary sanctuary of prayer on the hills and valleys at the crest of the Rockies.

A foundation was laid in those young childhood years that has served me well. Life has brought its hardship. At times I have been bewildered at the obstacles I have faced. But I could never get away from the memories of the depth of love I felt from God in those times of quiet anointing when he would fill my heart as a cup running over, leaving me with a sense of being loved that nothing on earth could match. Whenever I would begin to swerve off the path which would take me away from this Shepherd of Heaven, I would have such a sense of loss that I would run back into his arms. Those early years of my life, learning about the love God had for me personally, has created within me a passion for sharing the knowledge of this wonderful Shepherd with young children.

When our three children were very young, the church began a bus ministry. We would visit homes in the area, and on Sunday mornings would pick up the children. Sometimes they would still be in pajamas, and I am sure many of them had not had breakfast yet.

Many of these children had never been in church. Not everyone in the congregation was excited about these little children. Many times there would only be two or three of us ministering to about a hundred children. I was young, inexperienced, and with a scarce supply of teaching materials. There were times after a Sunday morning I would be completely spent. One morning at home when my own children were playing, I was praying about how I could teach those scruffy little children. The creative mind kicked in.

My first puppets were a choir of five, made from paper-mache. I cut my broom handle into five pieces, formed strange and goofy heads, painted them, designed choir robes and entered into a world of seeing God through the lens of young children. From that point our children's church had lions, dogs and human faces of many sorts. The ugliest puppet was Pink Baby, and of course, it was the favorite of the children.

When I was a young child, I would line my dolls up on the bed and care for them. I always wanted to be a mother, so my heart was blessed with our son and two daughters. When the bus ministry started, the demands that came with it were overwhelming and exhausting. It didn't take long for the realization to unfold within me of the faces of these children. I not only loved my own children, in fact I loved all children.

Throughout the week, I would be inspired to create materials made from everyday items around the home to enhance the Sunday morning Bible stories. Craig became involved with the puppets, and was one of my staunchest supporters when he was six years old. The experiences with those groups of children that came on buses every Sunday morning are a long ago memory, but everywhere I go I see the faces of children, and I am blessed. Looking back on that time, I pray that those little children grew up to know the Heavenly Shepherd.

Our church started a school which was named Fairlane Christian School. I have many rich memories of the years I taught there. One specific time comes to mind as I write this portion on the anointing. The prayers began in a classroom, and the intensity of seeking God spread throughout the school. This kind of moving of God's spirit cannot be orchestrated; it is a divine and sovereign anointing he pours out on those seeking him with all their hearts. As we prayed with the students, it was apparent that even very small children were being anointed as their faces took on a radiance that was from Heaven. Rachel and Shana were in the fifth and sixth grade at the time. As the children were gathered around praying, some of them stood and would preach to the others. As Rachel stood and began to preach, I just wept, knowing that the words she spoke had to come from a special anointing that would follow her throughout her life.

The children that experienced that powerful move of God in those days of prayer were forever changed. I would pray to God that all children would find themselves in a place where they could experience that kind of anointing while still young.

The anointing that is spoken of in the Psalms is what brings healing to the deepest wound. The oil of the Holy Spirit is what propels man into greatness as witnessed in the life of Stephen the Martyr and the Apostle Paul. God longs to pour out this same anointing on today's men and women and children if they will only seek him with all their hearts.

For I know the thoughts that I think toward you, says the Lord,
thoughts of peace and not of evil,
to give you a future and a hope.
Then you will call upon Me and go and pray to Me,
and I will listen to you. And you will
seek Me and find Me, when you search for Me
with all your heart.
Jeremiah 29:11-13 NKJV

God's voice comes to us in numerous ways. Many times the oil of anointing will come in the quiet of nature. I traveled a good deal while I worked for the university, so when I had the privilege of being home in Shell for the weekend, I was content and full of peace. I made sure I had gotten the grocery items needed so I wouldn't' have to go to town. I attended church on Sunday, but then I enjoyed my home with the pets. One blustery spring morning, I was enjoying a morning cup of coffee setting out on the deck. It wasn't unusual to see massive eagles flying up next to the mountain side where my home was situated. As I sat there relishing the quiet, I saw a huge eagle begin to circle around just out in front of the deck. The wing spread was enormous. My eyes were transfixed on this majestic bird. With each circle, the eagle would be propelled up higher into the clouds. In just a matter of moments I could no longer see the eagle. I sat there stunned at what I had just witnessed. I couldn't' help but think that is just what it's like when we allow the Holy Spirit to anoint us with his oil. We truly are taken to a place in the divine where we are so full of God's glory and magnificence that our cup runs over with his presence.

CHAPTER 12
OLD BARNS, SEWING, GARDENING, SHEPHERDS

Families who have that grandparent that preserves those stories from forever ago are fortunate. I have given each child and grandchild a copy of the homestead book. I really don't expect them to read it at this time but someday it will be on the shelf waiting for them. I consider it an honor that I was allowed to go back and preserve those family stories of those courageous homestead families who came to Wyoming in 1950.

Old Barns

Long after my father had passed away, on those rare times I was able to go back to the homestead, I would always make a point to go out and walk through those old lambing sheds.

There is something nostalgic about old barns no longer in use. For those of us growing up on farms or ranches, the barns were a place of work and necessity to protect the livestock. Our father did a great deal of work in building those old sheep sheds. They were long barns with dirt floors and lambing pens up next to the walls. It was silent as I walked down through the long shed. The only sounds I could hear were a few birds fluttering up in the rafters.

After I had grown up, I always felt like I was missing out on something, during the lambing season, knowing I was not able to see the little lambs frolicking out in the barnyard, feeding the bum lambs, or hearing my parent's stories of the sheep.

I have a chapter on Paint Creek Ranch in "Beloved Homeland, Growing up on a Wyoming Homestead.". The Hoffs became like our family in those early years and I could write volumes about Phyllis, six years older, then Mike and me. I think she was a hero for both of us. I was six and Mike was seven at the time. Even though this is not a very good picture I can see the mischief written all over my face. In later years when we would get together we could spend hours going back over our great adventures on Paint Creek Ranch.

I will share one of those snippets of writing of bringing back the memoires from Paint Creek Ranch of ever so long ago now.

Patty, Phyllis and Mike on Paint Creek Ranch

Memories of Paint Creek Ranch

The day was perfect. It was one of those Wyoming afternoons without a cloud in the sky. The sky was a deep set blue as I looked up and beyond the mountains. It was as if it would stretch on for eternity.

Felix, Phyllis, and I were sitting there by the river, watching it quietly move though an arid dry land.

Felix was almost 80 at the time. Years of ranching had etched its hand across his face with deep set furrows of life. By now Phyllis and I were grandmothers. Hard to believe how quickly the years had melted away. Each of us had memories that were as treasured as a priceless vintage.

    The old ranch just a few miles away held stories of the past. It was a child's fantasy land to my brother and me. We were best friends at six and seven. We could create worlds of wonder from the most basic elements.

    Years later when Felix and Bessie sold the ranch, I felt my childhood had been betrayed.

    As we sat there sharing treasured moments that have a quality only known by friendships carried over from another time and another generation, we decided to visit the old ranch.

    Paint creek was a very small stream that had wound its way around a large ravine which nestled under a wide plateau at the base of the Beartooth Mountains.

    As we drove across the flat rocky terrain, there was a melancholy air that settled down on each of us.

    We dropped down into the land of enchantment and the child in me wept way down inside in a quiet room no one could see.

    The meadows were still lush and green. Across the ravine were the hills with rock formations that could evoke wild and terrifying scenes for a child on horseback pursuing imaginary conquests.

    Up along the crevice was the old cave, which held secrets of stories, told long ago by three mischievous children.

    We reverently and silently climbed out of the car and stood on a threshold of overgrown weeds and grass where the foundation had been for the old log house.

    When the ranch was sold, the new owner had burned all the buildings to save on paying taxes.

    The old house was not a mansion mind you, but it was our fortress, our place in time, our keeper of holidays filled with laughter, music and loving friends.

    Much to my sorrow, the Hoffs always prepared lutefisk, a Scandinavian codfish tradition, on New Year's Eve.

I just couldn't help but feel a crime has been committed. How could a house so valuable be wiped away by such a thoughtless act? As if we could bring back the old logs stained with the seasons of life.

As we stood there, we each tried to remember just exactly where each room was located. We walked to the back of the house to the old willow tree. The fire had burned down all but a portion of the trunk.

So many times on those warm summer days I would climb into the arms of that old tree and share my secrets with Phyllis. Felix had anchored an old bed springs into the tall branches long before we had arrived on the scene.

Phyllis was a tall statuesque Swedish blond. I thought she was the most beautiful young woman in the world. She was all wise and kind; she could do no wrong.

It was upon the bed of springs, coupled with Phyllis's words of wisdom, Mike and I learned of life in its many facets. There were times the three of us found ourselves in a good deal of trouble with our parents, who somehow did not comprehend our zest for life, or maybe they did? It was at these times the mighty willow tree called to us. As we would ascend its mighty branches and sway back and forth, somehow our troubles were not so bad and we were safe to contemplate our next adventure.

As we stood together viewing the remains of a time gone by, we couldn't help but breathe a tribute to the willow tree, so faithful to us in another time.

We made our way across the creek and up a small bluff to the corral Felix had built. Most of the posts were still standing. The strong fence had held me many times as I would gaze upon the horses. We examined the moss that had crept into the wood as the years had come and gone. We decided we would have to talk to the owner and see if we could have a few of the logs.

As we moved away from the corral, we walked over to the old barn. We peered into the dark and dank building. There was a strand of sunlight that pierced through the dusty remains and smells of animals long dead now.

An object caught our eyes as we peered through the darkness. It was an owl glaring at us upon his perch. His face carried a defiant look of ownership, as if to say, "Go away, this is my home now, you are trespassing. The ranch you had is now just memories."

They were sad memories that afternoon, as some of our family members had gone on and we could not go back to that place in time. As we quietly walked down the hill, we each fought back tears, but we also felt a feeling of love and life and goodness in all the smells and sights, and sounds of yester-year, and so we were grateful we had shared all the feelings of goodness, sadness, joys and laughter once again.

Patricia McClaflin Booher, May, 1999

I am winding down to the last chapter of this second edition of the Shepherd book. I will have to admit I am very weary now. It seems that is the way it is in running a race, competing in a 4-H project or writing a book. When we can finally see the top of the mountain, the air seems to get thinner, but for those of us who are the climbers we just keep putting one foot in front of the other.

Very early on this cold January morning, I turned on my little electric franklin stove in my small alcove and said my prayers and wrote some notes for the day of writing. There was still a chill in the air so I went over to the rack and pulled out one of the quilts I had made for Mom in her later years.

I had hand stitched with embroidery thread the words, "I love you Mom." Such a small thing to do, but I am sure she looked at those words countless times and it brought peace to her heart, knowing of the love of her daughter.

I have a long list of grandchildren but really I see all children as special. Those years of teaching at Fairlane Christian School were some of the highlights of my own life.

I look back now on those many days of teaching and pray somehow those students knew they had a teacher that saw down into the hearts and cherished each one.

4-H SEWING PROJECT

When I returned to Wyoming and worked with UW Extension Service, I once again became involved with the 4-H program. Sewing was always my favorite project, so I was grateful I was able to take part in teaching the sewing leaders skills to help them in their projects. I planned many designing workshops for women throughout the county. I don't think I would have the energy for that now.

Down through the years I have acquired many skills in sewing, tailoring and designing. It would be hard to find classes for all of these many avenues of sewing I have had the privilege of learning.

When my granddaughters decided they wanted to join 4-H and have Grandma be their sewing leader I was over joyed. No moss grew under my feet, as I quickly went to Sandy and Craig and asked if I could be the girl's 4-H sewing leader.

I tend to wear rose colored glasses at crucial and pivotal points of life. The glasses came off quickly as the sewing projects began. My plan was to have regular meetings, allowing the girls time to sew with ease, no deadlines to be met, just a wonderful relaxing time with Grandma. If you are a parent of preteens, I can hear you laughing already. You know the score by now. How to fit one more activity into a household of five children would be a leap of faith.

There were many special moments with those two beautiful girls, but there were also long hours of instruction as I sat next to them teaching them the skills of sewing I had learned so many years ago from my mother and Edith Anderson, Park County Home Economist.

I would describe Edith and Niles Anderson as salt of the earth kinds of people. She passed away many years ago, but there have been many times I wished I could have gone to her and told her the profound impact she had on my life as she would become one of my life's heroes. When I came back to Wyoming and took a position with the UW Extension as an Extension Agent, I came to realize just how incredible that couple was.

Edith had salt and pepper hair, braided and neatly coiled in a bun at the back of her neck. She walked with a cane, but that didn't slow her down. She was a woman with a soft spoken voice that carried with it wisdom of experience and Godly Character. Niles worked alongside his wife, always ready to encourage and inspire young people.

Edith would give regular sewing classes to the 4-H leaders. I remember the day she taught me how to make bound button holes for my wool suit. She came to our home to personally examine the wedding dress I was designing for myself. So many memories come to mind of so long ago of a gentle quiet couple that inscribed on my heart that I was special.

I met Sandy and the girls in the parking lot of Jackson County fairgrounds on Tuesday morning. Many years of working at the county and state fair in Wyoming were behind me.

Elizabeth and Anna Booher at the fair with their sewing projects

. I wasn't going to be a sewing judge, or have to attend to the many tasks of running 4-H activities at a fair. I was Grandma, and I would stand back with their mother and watch, as the girls entered into a new experience of interview judging. They were nervous.

Would they remember what they were supposed to say? Would the judge be nice? Would she like their dresses? As it was time for each of the girls to step before the judge holding the dress they had worked on so carefully, it was as if Sandy and I were the only parents in the universe, as we watched both of them explain in detail what they had done and why. I could tell she was a good judge, she knew her stuff. They both received blue ribbons and we were all so proud of the accomplishment of the reward of sewing with excellence. Their father went on Saturday, so the girls could show their Papa the dresses on display in the showcase in the 4-H exhibit hall. Dads can be described as the icing on the cake, as the girls will long remember the look of pride on his face, just as I remember my father's face.

Gardening

Mom had tiny hands and feet, but that did not stop her from working alongside Daddy all those years. The homesteaders planted large gardens from the very beginning. In those early years we ate a lot of venison. The war veterans were starting a new life out on the prairies, sharing farm equipment, and working alongside each other. Families lived very frugally, but I think they all considered themselves very rich.

Summers were spent caring for the garden and then canning and freezing the produce. As I have grown older, I have often wished I had paid closer attention to Mom's gardening knowledge. I spent a lot of time out in the garden pulling weeds, but if I was working alongside Mom, I was chattering away like young children do, but I think that was important too. We didn't have air conditioning so late summer days in the kitchen canning hundreds of quarts of food was hot and tiring. The reward for the hard work was a great sense of accomplishment, as we looked at the jars of fruits and vegetables setting on the shelves out in the well house.

For many years when I was able to go back to Wyoming to visit my parents, I would bring home a jar of my mom's pickles as I needed them to make her special potato salad. After she passed away I was able to bring home the old crock she had used all those years. It is a special treasure to me of memoires of my mother. I have been practicing making those pickles and I think I am coming close to what she had made for over fifty years.

    The first time I had a garden and flowers in decorative pots on the deck was when I lived in Shell, Wyoming. It was a small garden but the vegetables were plentiful. The soil was rich up next to the mountains, although it was high desert. My friend and neighbor Linda Reed would help me with the watering when I would have to be off to the fairs in late August.

    When I came to the vintage home here in Michigan, the lady who had previously owned the home was very old. The back yard needed a great deal of work. Now, when I go back and see the pictures of that yard, it brings me pleasure as that was a project of pure pleasure for me every summer. I have many snippets of stories I wrote in those years and the topics often centered on my garden of vegetables and flowers.

Max, Dane and Luke Ross out in the garden patch

    When I moved to the apartment, the manger rototilled a garden plot out in the forest for me to have a garden. The soil was very poor and required a great deal of work, but I still took great pleasure along with the Ross grandchildren. We painted a rock city, made videos and on and on. We spent many hours out in the garden. I have a manuscript about the garden in the forest entitled, "Lessons of Life I Learned in my Garden Patch." I think I will take a time to regroup before starting again on that non-fiction novel.

Now that I am in my lake home, the soil is sandy. I planted many cucumber plants last summer, hoping to fill my crock with pickles but I was not very successful. There is always another year and another plan. At this point in my journey I think I will be happy with a variety of large ceramic pots with flowers on the deck and a few wooden boxes for vegetables.

My cottage has a large deck that looks out on the lake. I put a great deal of thought into the flowers, colors and sizes and shapes of the pottery taping into the creative part of my nature. I have even discovered a cherry tomato plant with the name of Rapunzel, so I have to say life is good.

Shepherds

The men out on the homesteads became close comrades in the farming adventures. They probably learned as much from the mistakes they made as the textbook knowledge they learned in those evening classes that were given to the Veteran farmers early on to assist them in developing the skills of irrigation farming. Such was the case with the families who raised sheep.

My Dad and Lloyd Snider shared farm equipment, worked along together and checked in with each other almost on a daily basis. The Sniders lived just around the corner up on the hill. The UW Agriculture Agents were regular visitors on the homestead farms, working with homesteaders, helping them with the many farming questions.

Lloyd and Dad were not only working partners, but the dearest of friends. I would characterize both of them as having Shepherds hearts, as they both cared for their flocks of sheep. Early in the morning after growing up, when going home, I would go to the sheep sheds with my Dad. Hopefully if I could go home while there were still ewes with their lambs out in the barnyard, I would hear the most delightful stories.

Daddy had names for many of the barn yard sheep. While working with the sheep day after day, he would observe the different temperaments and personalities. He used to tell the local pastor the sheep reminded him of congregations of people.

Looking back now on those growing up years, if I would have had an inkling that I would someday be trying to remember the everyday goings on out in the barn yard, would I have had the presence of mind to be making a journal about the day to day tasks that were so common place during that time? On a scale of animal intelligence, the sheep is not ranked at the top. In fact, sheep require a great deal of care. They are defenseless to protect themselves.

It is interesting that throughout the Bible man is likened to a sheep. Of course sheep were part of everyday life in those times, but is there deeper meaning in the similarities? A picture in reference to a story often taught in Sunday school is about the ninety-nine sheep in the fold.

From a shepherd girl's reflection I would see that the sheep have all been directed back into the pens for the night for protection. As the Shepherd counts, he discovers he is missing one small lamb.

Suppose one of you has a hundred sheep and loses one of them. Does he not leave the ninety-nine in the open country and go after the lost sheep until he finds it." And when he finds it, he joyfully puts it on his shoulders and goes home. Luke 15:3-5 NIV

He secures the latch on the gate and goes back out into the hills, although he is weary from a long hot day of herding the flock. He looks desperately as the sun sets to the west. In the distance he hears the bleating of the frightened little lamb. He rushes down the rocky cliffs, and takes the little lamb into his arms that has been stuck in a crevice of the rock. The lamb nestles down into the arms of the shepherd, as he knows he is safe. As the last rays of light pass over the horizon, the Shepherd is seen coming back to the enclosed pen holding the lamb. There is no bleating of this lamb now, as he knows he is coming home.

I am the good shepherd; I know my sheep and my sheep know me; just as the Father knows me and I know the Father, and I lay down my life for the sheep. John 10:14 & 15 NIV

Many years later when I returned to Wyoming, my father had been in Heaven for a number of years. I was able to see Lloyd Snider once in a while, which was always a pleasure, because it seemed he had a fragrance of life like my Dad possessed. The 4-H program had been such a vital part of the McClaflin family, so I felt I wanted to give back to this youth organization. Summers were filled with many activities in preparation for the county and state fair. Since our county fair was backed up to the state fair, getting all the exhibits labeled and prepared to transport in just a few days was a big task. After the first day of judging I spent most of the week in the 4-H barn. Those late summer afternoons in a cement block building with a metal roof were like being in a cooker.

By Thursday, I felt like a limp and welted piece of lettuce. My goal every year was to have the state fair exhibits labeled and ready to be boxed up before Thursday which was sheep judging day at the Big Horn county fair. The day began early as the judging would go on into the evening. After sheep judging there would be a contest called the "Sheep Lead." It was sponsored by sheep producers, with the intent of encouraging people to sew with wool. I had been asked to model a wool suit I had made. The late afternoon was sweltering and I was so busy, I didn't feel like putting on a wool suit, but I wanted to support what the wool growers were doing so I agreed to take part in the contest.

The Big Horn county fair is a community project. Compared to other counties, it was not so big in size, but I felt it was so down home. There were large trees that gave shade for the many activities throughout the week. It took a concerted effort on the whole community to conduct the fair.

One particular year that sticks out in my mind was the year I sat and watched the sheep judging with the fair manager, John Haley. By Thursday, my feet and legs ached so I would wear the most comfortable tennis shoes I had and hopefully I would be able to find a place to set down as I watched the judging. I had called my mother early asking her to come over to the Sheep Lead contest. No, actually I was tearfully begging her to come. I was so weary, and melancholy was moving in fast, I just didn't want to walk around in the Sheep Lead without her setting up there in the bleachers.

In the afternoon I came out of the 4-H exhibit hall and found a seat under one of the big trees. I was watching one of the classes of sheep being judged, when John Haley saw me and came over and sat down. He looked exhausted. I was tired, but I don't think my fatigue came close to his. As he sat there he began to talk about my dad. I looked at him, his face was red, and I could tell he was fighting back tears, as well as me. Oh dear, I wanted to hear what he said, so I listened carefully, as the ache in my chest increased. "Pat I remember your Dad and Lloyd Snider years ago when they came to judge the sheep contest at our fair. We started early in the morning, and the judging would go into the night. After the long day of judging, I would see your Dad over there in the sheep barn with 4-Hers talking to them individually, telling them what they could do the next year to improve their judging skills." There are times one just wants to roll the clock of time back, but we can't do that can we. He got up and walked away. After a while he came back again, telling me how much he respected my Dad and just how much he missed him.

I had to go back into the hot exhibit hall and keep working. I kept going to the back door looking for my mom's car. She didn't want to drive by herself, so she had Felix Hoff come with her. Bessie had died several years earlier of a stroke. The Hoffs were our close family friends so he would have understood my sadness on sheep judging day. When I saw them I walked out, just needing a hug, not wanting her to know how much my heart ached on that day.

Those times of working at fairs are behind me now. I don't know if I could keep up with that pace of work anymore. I am glad for those years of working with the 4-H program again but it is good to be here in Michigan with the grandchildren.

This is just a brief example of those homesteaders as they were so involved with each other and with the youth in our community. I tell the many stories of those dear friends who are no longer with us. As I look about society today, I am grateful that so many years ago that seed was planted in my heart to go back and document those wonderful stories of everyday life on the Heart Mountain homestead. Even though it was a challenge to prepare the manuscript and have it published in that first go around with Covid, I think I have some of that same grit and tenacity I was given as a child from my parents and community.

CHAPTER 13
SURELY GOODNESS AND MERCY

This morning, I find myself once again, excited and also intimidated at the same time. Will I ever advance past this complex set of emotions that are poles apart? Such is the life of the writer. Once, while attending a writing conference, I was listening very intently to the morning speaker who had completed several very distinguished books. She asked a question. "Why do we write?' And then she answered the question. "We write because we must write. That voice within each of us will not be satisfied, until those thoughts are written on the page." How true has been that experience in my own life. Thoughts begin to surface, and then multiply until I have this driving force that pulls me to my computer, and then my mind goes blank. When this happens, I have to rely on that discipline and knowledge that the Great Shepherd of Heaven will come, and when I feel weak and inadequate, he will become my strength. This is a scripture that has been a source of faith for me, in my own personal journey.

But he said to me "My grace is sufficient for you, for my power is made perfect in weakness." II Corinthians 12:9 NIV

As I placed my hands upon the keyboard today, I looked up to see the picture of my grandson Luke when he was four years old when my family and I went back to see my Mom.

I am so grateful when I look at Mitch, and realize how much he loves my daughter and their three boys. He not only loves his family, but takes on the role of protector, and makes family experiences special.

He had taken the time to make out a list of each thing that would happen on Luke's first plane ride.

When we were ready to depart from the Detroit airport, I looked across the aisle to see what the boys were doing.

Luke had put on a big plastic orange set of water goggles. I am not sure what the significance was to him, maybe a throwback to his children's collection of "Snoopy," but the goggles came on every time we were ready to begin another flight. Luke's choice of shoes during this season of his life were one blue shark and one green frog rubber boot.

The weekend past all too quickly. We were packing up getting ready to head back home, and Rachel wanted to take some pictures. Luke wanted Peeka, (his name for Grandma), to see the dirt road he had discovered. It was a cold blustery day with gray troubled clouds. On went the multi-colored boots, coat, and mittens, Max was snuggled down in warm blankets in his stroller and we were off. We went out to the north fields where the irrigation sprinkler was in sight. Luke began to walk down the deeply rutted path made by the huge tires that move in circular motion across the fields. Wayne had winterized the gigantic sprinkler machine and it set out in the field, silent waiting for spring. Mitch was navigating Max through the grass stubble, as we slowly made our way down to the old Alkali creek with its many memories of childhood.

I sit here today, once again studying this picture of one of my precious grandchildren. I remember how bravely Luke marched right into the northern winds, having a sense of place and family and confidence. He is a young man now but when his Grandma Peeka is in Heaven he will have stories of his great grandparents, Wallace and Edna Mae McClaflin, and their courage in facing life's challenges penned to the page. I think they would be so pleased to see this picture of Luke on the cover of "Beloved Homeland, Growing up on a Wyoming Homestead."

As I read through the stories penned on the pages of this manuscript, I am struck with the common every day memories I have related. Those circumstances and friendships that come along in one's life can aid in giving direction and purpose and make life a thing of value. When my brother Mike and his wife Linda were still making many missionary trips to Africa they sometimes would make a stop along the way at the International Airport in Detroit to see our family.

They both have a special place in the hearts of Craig, Shana and Rachel.

When they would come I knew they were weary from jet lag, but the schedule would be hectic as all of us wanted to spend time with them. On one such trip they were coming from Brussels and the flight was delayed for hours so they arrived very late at night. We had kept them up too late, but before they left, Mike called Reagan over to him. He took him up on his lap, and said, "Young man God has purposes for your life," and he prayed a blessing over that young man. That memory is indelibly printed on my heart and mind.

Uncle Mike McClaflin with Reagan Booher

He is a handsome young man now, but I still cherish this picture of little Reagan with one of the patriarchs of our family.

As the stories of Teddy and Ronnie have unfolded throughout this manuscript, I am realizing what a special blessing they have been to me personally. I asked Teddy to share with you about the home tours for children she and Ronnie conducted for a number of years. I am sure they could fill several books with the personal stories of the children through the years, but I penned just a brief overview for you.

LAMBING SEASON ON THE JONES FARM AND SCHOOL TOURS

There was a glow on Teddy's face as she began to recount those days with the children.

"For me it is so awesome to look at how God works in each and every one of our lives. God has used the sheep for Ronnie and me to be a way that we can share his love and bring to light how He cares for each and every one. If you look at the lambs and the ewes through lambing season when you go out into the sheep shed and see all the ewes bedded down you just have a feeling of God's presence there. Unknown to Ronnie and I, He has blessed us with the sheep and part of our way to pass this blessing on has been through the field trips for the young people in our area.

We had two purposes of having these field trips. One was to help young people to come back to the roots of the farm and see that you don't just go to the grocery store and buy everything.

There is a certain amount of work that needs to be done and also the role that agriculture plays in the food chain. The way we got started with this was with LeGene Vaughn who had a preschool. She always got so excited about the lambing season. She would bring the preschoolers and the class usually had about fifteen children. This was before the time of kindergarten in our local schools. She would come out with the children and they would spend about an hour. First of all what she wanted them to do was to have the joy and fun of feeding the orphan lambs and that is the way it got started.

Other teachers in the area heard about what was happening in the field trips from LeGene Vaughn. By word of mouth we soon had teachers from Powell, Lovell, Cody, Wapita and Clark School districts calling to know if they could have a field trip out to the farm.

Since our young people have been so far removed from agriculture Ronnie and I felt it was very important to introduce them to the facts and correct information concerning livestock. So over the twenty years of tours we would have approximately between 400-450 young people from kindergarten through 5th graders each year. Mostly kindergarten and 1st graders would come.

They would come and spend about 2-1/2 to 3 hours and we would take the young people through the process of feeding lambs. They would see how a baby lamb was born which was always such an excitement for the young people. They would observe how the lamb was incased in the sack, the fluids, how the baby lamb was so wet and slimy to the touch, how the baby took its first breath, how it got the first suckle of milk, the colostrum that is so important and how that baby started standing up.

And of course we had chickens. They would see the eggs being laid by the hens and feel the warmth of the eggs. They would also have the opportunity to experience milking a goat which was a new experience for many. Not only were we reaching the young people, many parents would come because they had never seen the birthing process. The children's eyes would just get big when they would see that little nose and little tongue come out for the first sign of birth. We especially had one little boy that got so excited that he got right down there beside Ronnie and he was wanting to pull on that baby lamb. Ronnie let him help pull the lamb out which we did with all the boys and girls. But he was just into the whole birthing process and when he was done the teacher handed him a napkin to wipe his hands off so he could participate in the feeding of the lambs and some other activities like the branding and numbering and this kind of thing, docking and castrating of the lambs. The teacher informed us that he took that napkin home and his mother had to put it in a scrapbook and the last I knew it was still there.

One other result of having the field trips is that we had one teacher who brought an autistic child and she was very frightened of all the noises and all the smells and everything. We worked with that child and finally got her where she would touch a baby lamb and actually hold the bottle while a lamb was nursing which was a tremendous breakthrough. Later on the teacher reported back that the child had never spoken any words whatsoever and after the experience out on the field trip to the lambing farm, she did speak a few words so they felt that played an important role in the breakthrough for the child with autism.

So you can see that God had His hand in many things even though, as we were doing the field trips we did not really realize how God was working and how God was using the lambs and using us to help share what He had given us. It has always been a highlight in our lives. We still have young people which are out of school now or some may be out of college in fact come out and say we remember when we came out to see the lambing at your house. I'll have mothers say, "Are you the people that had the field trips?" So they are still recalling it as a wonderful experience and it was all because of God. He has given us the sheep to share and to help see the joy and realize that humans are really no different than sheep. They need the love, they need the tender care, and they need the guidance just like we do from our Heavenly Shepherd.

One other side note is that these little children were so lovable, so adorable and so innocent. We would be in the process of a ewe having a baby and they would just really be watching and observing what was happening. We had one little girl whose eyes were just as big as saucers. We had this ewe pushing her baby lamb out and she was in the cheering section on the side with those big, big beautiful eyes of hers and she was saying to the ewe, "Push girl, push, come on girl, push!" Oh my goodness when that baby came out there was just all sorts of shouts of joy and it was just such an exciting time to see how God has used all his creation to help us see Him.

Preparing for the field trips was a challenge because we wanted to make sure that everything was in order. We wanted the sheep shed to smell very good so that when the boys and girls would walk in they wouldn't go "ooh, ick." We wanted a good odor. We didn't want a lot of manure so they would get it on their shoes. So it took quite a bit of work to keep the barn clean. We had to have everything covered with straw. If we had a lamb that died during the night, it would have to be taken care of. We did not want these young ones to see the dead lambs or anything like that. We started early in the morning because we would have boys and girls arriving about nine o'clock and they would be with us until a quarter to twelve. Through that time we went into the shed and made sure that all the pens were strawed, watered and fed. Where they came in, we would set down straw bales in a semi-circle so they could see everything. And of course being there for a couple of hours these little ones would get pretty hungry so we always had cookies and some kind of a drink like hot chocolate or something prepared so that they could have refreshments.

 Many times we would get thank you notes back from the children and I would think oh my goodness what did we teach because it would be the cookies that they thought was the highlight of their trip that day. But as they grew older and as I would hear reports back from mom and dad it was the lambing they remembered. This was such a wonderful opportunity because we had parents that would come with their children. We ran two classes a day; one in the morning and one in the afternoon. We would start the morning class about nine to about a quarter to twelve and the second class, one to about a quarter to three. So that was sort of our schedule for the day and many times we would have anywhere from ten children to fifty children per group.

 Usually we would have about one parent for every four or five children, so we were also reaching a lot of the moms and dads and they used this as an opportunity for over the supper table to talk about a lot of things; about the birthing process, about caring for animals and responsibilities. It just opened up the door for a lot of dialogue in families, which here again, God was working even though I did not realize it. As I look back I can see a lot of things that God had His hand in. Just helping us to get everything ready in time for all those kids and to give us the strength and energy was a blessing. As I said we had about 450 boys and girls go through that lambing shed in those field trips each year and we did it in approximately a 2 to 2 1/2 week period and we did this for twenty years."

 I knew of the tours to the Jones farm through the years, but until I sat across from Teddy that afternoon listening to her, I never realized before what dedication this farm couple had in giving so much to the young children of that community for so many years.

The Voice of the Shepherd

Throughout my personal story I have shared with you, I have spoken of that soft voice that many times comes with the wind. The message that comes is clear and sometimes a great deal of faith and courage is needed to answer the call of God's spirit. And now you the reader might be asking, how could I possibly come to a place that I could hear this same Shepherd of Heaven. Actually He is speaking to you all the time.

I wish that I could tell you that life becomes easier, but it would be a lie. Through a process of living, we learn our lessons and hopefully we learn them well. One important lesson of life for me is that I know I can trust the Heavenly Shepherd to do right by me. Time and again I have found that the Lord does want to bless humanity with goodness and mercy spoken of in Psalm 23. I think of Corrie Ten Boom and Mother Theresa. Their lives were not of comfort and ease as they had great struggles, and yet God's mercy and grace shown so brightly through their lives. I am sure in the many years of hard work and labor, Teddy and Ronnie did not realize that one day they would share with you and me the special Godly wisdom that has followed them throughout life.

You might be saying at this point, what do these stories have to do with me? I live in the city, and I have never even held a lamb. I will ask you to think for a moment. What are those dreams buried down in you? What purposes in life have been laid out for you that if fulfilled you would have a sense of great joy and worth. I will have to say, I have spent many late nights working on this manuscript. At times I have felt a bit overwhelmed, but with all the discipline and work has come a joy so wonderful I can hardly contain it at times.

In living out that destiny God has for each of us, we not only have a sense of worth, but we can encourage another to walk in the paths of goodness and mercy.

Praise be to the God and Father of our Lord Jesus Christ, the Father of compassion and the God of all comfort, who comforts us in all our troubles, so that we can comfort those in any trouble with the comfort we ourselves have received from God.
II Corinthians 1:3 & 4 NIV

CHAPTER 14

AND I WILL DWELL IN THE HOUSE OF THE LORD FOREVER

When I look back over this journey that is called life, my heart is full of gratitude for the rich tapestry of color and beauty that has followed me all of my days on earth. I can't remember when I began to love this Shepherd of Heaven, maybe forever?

The shepherd book was first published in 2009. It took a great deal of soul searching as I was working on the Qualitative Research project that would evolve into the historical novel, "Beloved Homeland, Growing up on a Wyoming Homestead."

Last spring after surviving months of walking through Covid, I was thankful I would be able to see another spring.

I have had countless life experiences where it took a great deal of faith and grit, but the outcome was a resiliency and appreciation for life. As I recovered I slowly began to finish the manuscript of my Yorky pet, Timmy and tools for coping with grief.

So now, once again in a very cold January I am sitting in my office looking out on a frozen lake, writing and editing day after day with a second edition of the Shepherd book.

I have often quoted something I heard spoken by Sheila Walsh, "Don't die before you are dead," I think that has become my motto for living.

I am coming close to eighty now and I don't think in my lifetime I have witnessed such a degree of fear, anger and division that seems to invade every avenue of living. It would be easier to just sit back and let things roll, but I have grandchildren and I would say I love all of humanity. What could I possibly do to make a difference/

I remember my granddaughter, Anna, praying for me as I was recovering from the concussion. It was a perplexing time as I did not know how life would turn out for me after the accident. She prayed with such power and love over me. "Grandma, you are going to end well!"

That day so long ago now, out in Shirley Basin, in Wyoming, as I drove into a brutal snow storm I was quoting the 23rd Psalm. I had just said, "And I will dwell in the house of the Lord forever and forever and forever." I thought I would see God that day, but my destiny had not been completed. It will be a beautiful day when I do see Jesus face to face and my parents and oh so many others I have loved. But for now, I will pen these stories of triumph through all of life's experiences.

I am the Alpha and the Omega, the First and the Last,
the Beginning and the End.
Blessed are those who wash their robes, that they may have the right
to the tree of life and may go through the gates into the city.
Revelation 22:13-14 NIV

As I have allowed myself time to reflect on those childhood experiences of walking with this Shepherd of Heaven, it is with a thankful heart I pen these final thoughts. One of my favorite stories in the Old Testament is of Caleb, going to spy out the Promised Land. It was a discouraged group of men who came back to meet with Moses. They saw the giants in the land they had been promised and their hearts were full of fear. But then there was Caleb who had another spirit. I am sure if you and I would have the opportunity to follow this man on his journey of life, he had learned to know the voice of this Shepherd in the hard times, so that when he was faced with giants to conquer, Caleb knew God would be with him.

"But because my servant Caleb has a different spirit and follows me
wholeheartedly, I will bring him into the land he went to, and his
descendants will inherit it." Numbers 14:24 NIV

During my time of working with UW Cooperative Extension, the highlights of those years were the times Teddy and I worked together.

We both had an innate love for children, and people in general, so we drew energy from each other. One of the programs that comes to mind dealt with "Anger Management." After presenting the program a number of times, we pulled together the resource materials that most related to audiences and then we settled on a name, "Tiger in Your Tank." One particular three-week session we taught was with a group of high risk young people from the ages of ten to sixteen. It was not an easy assignment, but we worked together to reassure these youngsters. After the last session, we spent a few minutes allowing the participants, to give us some feedback. One sixteen-year-old gentleman raised his hand. "After taking this class, I believe I am going to be able to take control of my raging temper, and I think I will be able to have a life now." A hush fell over the group, as each person in that room knew the courage it took for that young man to be so honest. When the room was put back in order, and the lights were turned out, Teddy and I went out to the parking lot and said Goodbye. We both felt an incredible peace, knowing young people had walked away from those sessions with a hope for the future.

I acquired many excellent resources along the way on resiliency. I am so grateful that I had the privilege of working with Dr. Ben Silliman, UW Family Life Specialist, as he was very instrumental in introducing me to many resources on resiliency that have enriched my life and I have applied to many programs. I attended a seminar on "Hurting Children," with Ruth Arent, MA, MSW. She had done extensive work with hurting children. Fortunately I brought home a resource manual, "Trust Building with Children Who Hurt." It was chucked full of materials I would use in the coming years. One particular resource came from years of documented research for the difference between "Children Who Hurt", and "Children Who Hate."

Because Teddy and I worked mostly in a secular setting, we knew we needed to use wisdom. But when it was time for me to relate to the issue of hurt verses hate Teddy would step back and let me take all the time needed. I would look into the faces of those in the audiences and I would feel such deep compassion for them. I would tell them I didn't want to offend anyone, but one of the greatest gifts I had found in life was knowing that God would give me the ability to forgive. I could come through any storm, because I knew regardless of how weak I felt, or how angry, I could count on the Great Shepherd of Heaven to come and fill my heart with love, so that I could go on in life's journey and have peace and hope for a future and be filled with mercy and grace all the days of my life.

We conducted many seminars together, with all kinds of groups and settings of people. This was a poem I had penned during that time of working which we used to bring a closure to the programs we presented and I still refer back to the words often even after all these years. . .

CHOICES

The longer I walk through this journey of life,
I realize the power I possess within to make choices,
Choices daily,
Sometimes minute by minute.
Great personal courage and faith at times are necessary,
When I make choices where there are sacrifices,
When I choose love over hate,
When I choose forgiveness over holding on to unforgiveness,
When I choose to look beyond myself
To see that one who needs my caring.
Yes, life is a choice.
So soon my days will pass.
What will I leave behind?
Dear God, give me the courage to choose goodness.
Patricia, October 22, 1996

Life is full of choices that come with each day, sometimes they come moment by moment, but God is mindful of our cry, when we need that added boost of courage. I am sure the reason I have always had such a deep love for children is because I have been very aware from childhood that knowing this Shepherd so early in life was a great privilege.

When I hear of a young person committing suicide, it always brings a grief to my soul. What a sense of loss it is to know they will never have the opportunity to soar with eagles wings or see a little robin red breast with a wounded wing fly off into the morning sunlight.

I never have believed in the generation gap because it is not in the season of life we find ourselves that makes the difference, it is that innate ability to look beyond ourselves and to truly love that other person regardless of age, rank or serial number. There is something so special when we find that person who just loves us unconditionally, who stands in the wings and cheers us on, who has the time to listen, who reassures us regardless of circumstance that we have a future and a hope.

I wanted to share with you the reader, this testimony given by Ronnie of his own personal walk with God. It is so filled with truth, honesty and tenderness.

"Sheep have played a big role throughout my life. They are a rewarding animal. They will try to stay away but they still have trust in you especially as they get to know you better. As I think about my life I have been like the sheep as I knew the Lord early on when I was young but then I worked for my own self thinking I could do my own thing and so consequently drifted away from the Lord just like the sheep might stray from the shepherd. I never got into a lot of trouble but I could have. Of course sheep are the same way as they drift away and move into a hollow away from the shepherd in search of food and maybe a better pasture that appears to be greener. When I looked at myself as a human, I probably thought the same thing. And then as I think about coming back closer to the Lord I realize the safety and self-assurance the Lord gives me. I'm kind of like Moses; I drifted around for about 40 years where I didn't really keep the Lord completely away and I often thought of the Lord but I wasn't actively engaged with Him.

I came to a time I wished to know the Lord more closely, so for about the last ten years I have come to know him more deeply. I watched my wife Teddy who was coming to know the Lord more closely, even before myself. She kept wanting me to also enjoy that presence of the Lord. We became closer to the Lord through a program in a local church in which we became involved.

As we participated in the Bible teaching program we also became closer to the Lord and I feel that I found the Lord Jesus and gave my soul over to Him. As I continue my life I find a lot of peace and comfort in knowing the Lord and knowing that He is my personal savior and that I will be able to be with Him at my life's end. I find comfort in this, knowing that God has given me that grace and the chance that I will be with Him forever throughout eternity."

As I reached over and turned off the tape recorder, it was quiet in that kitchen, as I realized I had just heard the heartfelt words of a kindly shepherd man who had come full circle and life had taken on a depth and purpose as the Great Shepherd of Heaven had come into a clear focus in Ronnie Jones.

I have often referred to the work done by Erik Erikson in relation to the eight stages of life. In the eighth and final stage of life, "Integrity verses Despair," I have penned a quote that parallels what we are relating in reference to living with purpose. "Only in him who in some way has taken care of things and people and has adapted himself to the triumphs and disappointment adherent to being, the originator of others or the generator of products and ideas-only in him may gradually ripen the fruit of these seven stages." Erikson, page 269

I have known individuals who have lived their last days on this earth in great despair. At times I have been asked to attend a person's funeral, so that there would be someone setting in the audience. And then I have attended funerals where there was great sadness, as the individual had given such an investment to others that their passing on to be in Heaven would leave a great vacancy. They had completed this journey of life with great integrity. They had left a rich inheritance to those they loved. As I again look at the picture of my grandson heading into the wind, walking in the deeply furrowed path on the old homestead where I had my roots, my prayer is that my life has planted many seeds of righteousness for future generations of humanity.

Now I commit you to God and to the word of his grace, which can build you up and give you an inheritance among all those who are sanctified. Acts 20:32 NIV

As we come to know this Shepherd of Heaven, we gain an assurance that he is like that rock I would set on in the late summer days in Shell canyon. His is not moved or shaken by the affairs of man, but looks with great compassion on each of us.

The Lord has promised that he will never leave us nor forsake us and the Bible tells you and me that if we accept him, when our life is ended we will be with him forever and forever and forever.

Do not let your hearts be troubled. Trust in God; trust also in me. In my Father's house are many rooms; if it were not so, I would have told you. I am going there to prepare a place for you. And if I go and prepare a place for you, I will come back and take you to be with me that you also may be where I am. John 14:1 – 3 NIV

But our citizenship is in heaven. And we eagerly await a Savior from there, the Lord Jesus Christ, who, by the power that enables him to bring everything under his control, will transform our lowly bodies so that they will be like his glorious body."
Philippians 3:20 NIV

A Sense of Time and Place, "Community"

I know so well the time is winding down and the last words of this story must come to a close, as this is not just my story of the 23rd Psalm. Down through the ages of time the words in this short chapter of Psalms have brought comfort and also times of triumph of overcoming to generations.

Some times in those quiet moments I have treasured with the family one-on-one we have had those deep down in the heart conversations. In the world of movies, with the death of the older family member, everyone gets to be there as they whisper their last words this side of eternity. It is heart breaking to realize in the last several years with the pandemic of Covid, many loved ones were locked away in isolation for months and died alone away from family.

I don't know how it will all work out for me, but if you were to ask me what few words would be your last spoken to those you love more than life.

I would say, above all else, "Get Character." On a regular basis, check to make sure you are living within the guide lines of this scripture.

> *He has shown you, O man, what is good;*
> *And what does the Lord require of you*
> *But to do justly,*
> *To love mercy,*
> *And to walk humbly with your God?*
> *Micah 6:8, NKJV*

To say that life was easy out on those wind swept prairies of northern Wyoming would not be the truth. Beginning from the basic elements with a whole new group of families to have a healthy and thriving community took a great deal of hard work, pure grit and a lot of goodness. No matter what topic I approach with writing, the reader will always recognize that thread of a "sense of time and place."

I will share one memory of those first years on the homestead. The families had a community club house which was made of up of four barracks from the Japanese Internment Camp. Oh, it was not fancy. The men and women worked very hard sharing the dedication of fixing it up to be presentable. One spring in those early years we had a talent show. My mother took me to town and we went to the Bonner's Five and Ten to find sheet music. Although we still did not have electricity out in our Heart Mountain community, some of the neighbors had battery operated radios. The song at the top of the charts was "Dear Hearts and Gentle People."

I remember my mother working with me for days practicing, telling me I could sing the song. When I stood up in front of that group of neighbors, I was just so scared, but when I looked at their faces, I saw such love for me that I just began to sing with this lyric soprano voice I am sure I inherited from my Mom. When I went back so many years later and would sit in the kitchen with those neighbors who had carved out such a wonderful community giving the children a "sense of time and place," that same look of love came back to me.

Dear Hearts and Gentle People

I love those dear hearts and gentle people
Who live in my home town
Because those dear hearts and gentle people
Will never ever let you down

They read the good book from Fri' till Monday
That's how the weekend goes
I've got a dream house I'll build there one day
With picket fence and rambling rose.
I feel so welcome each time that I return
That my happy heart keeps laughing like a clown
I love those dear hearts and gentle people
Who live and love in my home town.

In the last few years, singing with that lyric soprano voice has been difficult from bouts of pneumonia. For several months, Covid had so affected my lungs that it was hard to speak and I could not sing at all, which was a bit discouraging. I was not able to attend church for months, but was happy I could listen to the service on the Internet. I really wanted to attend the Good Friday service, but knew I was still so weak. I stepped out in faith and had my daughter Shana and her husband pick me up for the service, I was happy to be out again with family and friends. The worship team began to sing a song I had not heard before, "Rattle." I was so inspired by the words and felt that strength from God's spirit welling up within my chest. I began to sing for the first time in months. And yes, with pure joy I was singing in that high pitched lyric soprano voice I had not heard come from me in a long time.

When I first began to write those first poems on that winter day looking out on the Big Horn Mountain range, with heavy snow coming down, and my faithful little dog sleeping beside my chair, courage was required to pen the first words. And then rapidly the words came with one poem after another. And so my friend, I have shared with you some of my sorrows, but more than that stories of a rich inheritance filled with much joy and peace given to me from my family and friends, and most of all from the Heavenly Shepherd who is so dear to my heart. I must now bring closure to this part of many more stories that will follow, and so I will go to that quiet place where poems come to mind.

PASSAGE

You there standing by the sidelines,

Thinking your time has passed you by,

The comfort of a warm room setting next to the fire

brings solace,

But only for a short time.

Those questions on your mind,

What if? What if?

Though your gray hair is now turning to shades of

glistening white,

Can you not go back and remember your stories of life

for the young ones.

Don't pass them off as the reckless generation

for they have great promise.

They have many challenges before them.

Your smile of encouragement will give them
wings to fly.
Just as the eagle taking flight in the blustery clouds of
northern skies,
Or a precious grandchild heading into to the wind in a
deep rut of soil
From many years of life's experience
You have choices that can make an impact long after
you are asleep.
Will you give hope and integrity, or will your message
be one of despair.
The Great Shepherd of Heaven calls you now,
To that quiet place where he will give you wisdom of
rare beauty
That you can pass on to the young ones.
Not everyone has been given the privilege of coming
Into this season of life.
Many others died young on a battlefield
far from home.
Some were taken early from the
ravages of cancer,
But you dear friend can pass on a
rich heritage,

So get up now and be about the task of living.

Take the hand of a young child.

Bless life and all its goodness.

But most of all be thankful.

Patricia, December 2008

Luke Ross walking on the north field of the Wyoming homestead

"All your children shall be taught by the Lord,

And great shall be the peace of your children."

Isaiah 54:13

FUTURE BOOK TO BE RELEASED

CHILDREN'S STORY

"HERE, LAMBY, LAMBY, LAMBY"

When this project first began, it was early in January. I was planning on writing children's curriculum for our church mission team who would be traveling to Kenya, East Africa in the summer. I had chosen the 23rd Psalm which, for many reasons, is very close to my heart. In just a matter of a few weeks, I realized I had been away from the lambing sheds for too many years, and I needed to refresh my knowledge of caring for orphan lambs.

I booked a flight to Wyoming to spend a few days on the old homestead with Mom and visit childhood friends, Teddy and Ronnie Jones, who still have flocks of sheep.

I took a friend along, Virla Harrell, who is a watercolor artist. She had helped me with the transcripts of interviews with homesteaders which would be documented in the non-fiction novel, "Beloved Homeland, Growing up on a Wyoming Homestead. "

By the time I could leave my work and travel to Wyoming, the lambing season was almost over. I didn't know if there would be any newborn lambs for us to see. As we drove up to the farmhouse Teddy met us with a smile on her face with news that a Suffolk ewe had given birth to triplets early that morning. There were two other orphan lambs Teddy was caring for in the farm house that would become the two main characters of the children's story.

Virla painted a watercolor picture of Ronnie holding, one of the triplets, we named Sammy. This picture would make its way to Africa with the 23rd Psalm written in English and Swahili in a laminated overly.

The story of the triplets and the two wounded lambs we named Bo and Susie would have to become a children's story.

Susie and Bo from the Lamby Story

This is actually a true story of little lambs that had been wounded and were fortunate to have been born on the Jones farm. The interviews taken from transcripts from conversations with Teddy and Ronnie about their life long vocation of caring for sheep and their love of the 23rd Psalm weaves a beautiful story relating to two wounded lambs. The title of the children's story comes from the way Teddy would call her orphan lambs to her out in the barn yard at feeding time, "Here, Lamby, Lamby, Lamby."

Day after day as I would write the story, I would see before me faces of little African children in the worst of situations. We were going to an area where the death rate from disease was high, and many children were left as orphans.

Each week I would take the chapter I had written and share it with the children at church. We all grew to love these three little lambs.

One day when I called to check on the three little lambs, Teddy had to tell me Bo died. When I got off the phone, I couldn't understand why I felt such sadness over an orphan lambing dying. That week as I read the next chapter of the lamby story to the children, we all cried.

I wondered how I would be able to write about Bo dying, but the Great Shepherd of Heaven would impress on my heart that I was going to a faraway place where death was an everyday occurrence. He wanted to reassure those little children that he loved them.

Along with writing the story of Bo and Susie, I made puppets which were left with the children in Africa.

Our team traveled to Africa and shared with the beautiful children there the story of the 23rd Psalm and of Bo and Susie. There were throngs of children and even now as I write their faces are imprinted on my mind and spirit. Each evening we would have the children make a line and we would pass out the little picture of the Wyoming shepherd holding Sammy with an inscription of the 23rd Psalm overlaid to stay with each of them, long after the mission team had returned home.

Several years later, Ben Poxson, one of the team members from the first mission trip returned again to the same location in Africa. One evening after a long day of building a church he was entering the hotel where we had previously stayed. A young school girl saw him from across the street. She called to Ben and ran over and got into her back pack. She pulled out the little lamented picture of Sammy the lamb with the inscription of the 23rd Psalm written in Swahili. What a thrill to hear after so much time those words of the 23rd Psalm were with this young girl.

And so here is the story of a triplet named Sammy, who narrates the story of two little orphan lambs who became great friends. After the death of Bo, Susie missed him terribly, but soon she was taken back to the sheep sheds where she looked for other little orphan lambs that needed her care. This is a children's story of inspiration; a story of friendship and courage.

But Jesus said, "Let the little children come to Me, and do not forbid them; for of such is the kingdom of heaven." Matthew 19:14 NKJV

FAMILY PHOTO ALBUM

Wallace and Edna Mae McClaflin

Mom, Mike and myself at Paint Creek Ranch with Lady and Nosy

Wallace McClaflin, Photography by Laing, Powell, Wyoming

Wayne, Mike and Patty McClaflin

Pam and Wayne McClaflin

Edna Mae McClaflin, Pam McClaflin, Rachel Ross, Max Ross, Patty McClaflin, Mitch Ross, Luke Ross, Wayne and Mike McClaflin on the Wyoming homestead with Heart Mountain in the background

Patty and Linda McClaflin on Mackinaw Island trip

Wayne & Pam McClaflin under the old apple tree on the homestead

Patty with her mom, Edna Mae McClaflin

Edna Mae McClaflin's 90th birthday celebration

Fall visit to Meckley's orchard with Sandy, Patricia and Craig Booher

Son Craig and Sandy Booher by their pond next to the

"Booher Market and Italian restaurant"

Craig Booher speaking at Napoleon Baccalaureate

Great granddaughter Claire with her grandmother, Sandy Booher

Erik and Alyssa Booher

Erik Booher and Perry Lewis

Elizabeth Booher and Grandma

Devin and Anna Otto

Great granddaughter Claire with her mother Rachel

John Booher and daughter Claire

Regan Booher at McCourtie Park

Grandchildren at Hidden Valley Park

Paul and Shana Lewis

Perry Lewis, Grandma, Kam and Gabe Lewis at Erik and Alyssa's Wedding

Kam Lewis

Kam and Kassie Lewis

Gabe Lewis, Property of P.E.L. Photography

Luke Ross, Grandma and Perry Lewis

Perry Lewis, Property of P.E.L. Photography

Lake Michigan, Luke Ross, Gabe and Perry Lewis

Mitch and daughter Rachel Ross on the Wyoming homestead

Mitch and Rachel Ross on African Safari

Mitch &Rachel Ross, Mike, Patty & Linda McClaflin in Nairobi, Kenya

Ross and McClaflin families at Grand Hotel on Mackinac Island

Dane, Luke and Max Ross with Grandma

Dane Ros

Max, Dane and Luke Ross

Luke Ross, B Marie Photography

Max Ross

Dane Ross

The Years Roll Back

Perry, Luke and Reagan sitting on the cement bench in the garden with Pom Poms hats from Grandma Preschool

Grandchildren making bread at Grandma's home

Thanksgiving day with three generations of family

Grandchildren always loved to sit on the cement bench

Summer days at Van Buren State Park on Lake Michigan. This is the famous noodle fight with Gabe Lewis, his mother, Shana Lewis, Mary Danko, Perry Lewis and Luke Ross. Notice all other swimmers have fled and Grandma is on shore taking the picture.

This is one of the first and rare pictures taken when the McClaflin family came to their new homestead home in Wyoming in front of the barracks. Mike and Patty McClaflin

Patricia in Maasia Mara Game Reserve in Kenya, East Africa

This has always been one of my favorite hymns, as this so describes the journey I have had from the time I was a young child. From the mountain tops and even in the valleys, I have called my Saviour Blessed.

BLESSED ASSURANCE

Blessed assurance, Jesus is mine! Oh, what a foretaste of glory divine!

Heir of salvation, purchase of God, born of His Spirit, washed in His blood.

This is my story, this is my song, praising my Saviour all the day long

This is my story, this is my song, praising my Saviour all the day long.

RESOURCES

BIBLE REFERENCES

New International Version, NIV

New King James Version, NKJV

Resource Books

Arent, Ruth P., MA, MSW. <u>Trust Building With Children Who Hurt</u>. The Center for Applied Research in Education, West Nyack, New York, 1992, Page 2.

Curran, Dolores, <u>Traits of a Healthy Family</u>. Ballantine Books, New York, 1983.

Erik Erikson, <u>Childhood and Society</u>. W.W. Norton and Company, New York, 1963.

Kubler-Ross, Elisabeth and David Kessler, <u>On Grief and Grieving: Finding the Meaning of Grief through the Five Stages of Loss</u>. Scribner, New York, 2005

Stoltz, Paul G. <u>Adversity Quotient Turning Obstacles into Opportunities</u>. John Wiley and Sons, Inc. New York, 1997. Pages 18-20.

Warren, Rick, <u>The Purpose Driven Life</u>. Zondervan, Grand Rapids, Michigan, 2002.

Woolen, Steven, M.D. and Sybil Wolin, Ph.D. <u>The Resilient Self, How Survivors of Troubled Families Rise Above Adversity</u>. Villard Books, New York, 1994.

Songs

Blessed Assurance. Fanny Crosby lyrics, melody by Phoebe Knapp, 1873.

Dear Hearts and Gentle People, Sammy Fain, Music and Bob Hilliard, Lyricist, 1049.

In the Garden, Lydia Baxter, 1809 – 1874, William H. Doane, 1832 – 1915, Gospel Publishing House, Springfield, Missouri, 1969.

It is Well with My Soul, Horatio G. Spafford, 1828 – 1888, Philip P. Bliss, 1838 – 1876, Gospel Publishing House, 1969.

BOOK ORDER INFORMATION

Photo by "A Pair of Photographers" www.apairphoto.com

Patricia McClaflin Booher weaves a tapestry of life experience, mingled with aspects of creativity, family resiliency and faith in her stories. The outcome brings a sense of time and place across generational lines. She received an M.S. degree in Human Resources, Family and Child Development from Eastern Michigan University.

To find information for books and journals go to:

www.patriciamac.com and Amazon.com

"Reflections of a Wyoming Shepherd on the 23rd Psalm,"

Second Edition

Soft Cover   E-Book

"Beloved Homeland, Growing up on a Wyoming Homestead"

Soft Cover   E-Book

"Timmy the Timid, Timmy the Tender,"

Tools for Coping with Grief

Soft Cover   E-Book

Journal for Quiet Moments

Quilter's Writing and Design Journal

Journal of Recipes and Memories

Wyoming Roots," Planner and Writing Journal

Books to be released in the near future

"Here Lamby, Lamby, Lamby," Children's Book

Creativity, "Beauty Unfolding"

"Lessons of Life I learned in my Garden Patch"

Rock Pavilion Press LLC

www.ingramcontent.com/pod-product-compliance
Lightning Source LLC
Chambersburg PA
CBHW060352110426
42743CB00036B/2769